THE 1876

YELLOWSTONE

EXPEDITION

CATASTROPHE AT THE LITTLE BIGHORN

AND

HUNTING SITTING BULL

BY GENERAL JOHN GIBBON

Originally published in the American Catholic Quarterly Review

1877

COPYRIGHT 2014 BIG BYTE BOOKS

DISCOVER MORE LOST HISTORY AT BIGBYTEBOOKS.COM

Contents

PUBLISHER'S NOTES

Primary sources must always be read within the context and time that they were written. General John Gibbon's 1877 articles, written only one year after the disaster of Little Bighorn, are no exception.

Gibbon was part of General Alfred Terry's Yellowstone Expedition in 1876 to round up the Sioux, Cheyenne, and other tribal members who were refusing to return to their reservations. Of course, the most famous member of this expedition was Lieutenant-Colonel (Breveted General) George Armstrong Custer, commanding the 7th Cavalry forces.

General Gibbon was first in the field and was camped on the north bank of the Yellowstone River at the mouth of Rosebud Creek. Though Lieutenant James Bradley and scouts of Gibbon's command had seen a large Native American encampment of possibly 300 lodges up the Rosebud (Gray, 1991), Gibbon appears to have minimized this in reports to Terry. Gibbon does not mention the encampment in these articles.

Nevertheless, Gibbon's account of the campaign is very valuable and readable. Like many of his contemporaries, he found much to admire about his Native American opponents and like many military men, felt that the problems created between whites and Indians had to do with broken treaties and white incursion on land promised to Indians. The military, in his mind, was merely the obedient executor of a policy set in Washington by Grant, Sherman, Sheridan and politicians, and a protector of whites moving into the region.

Terry and Gibbon's approach to the Little Bighorn Valley from the west probably saved Major Marcus Reno's troops on June 26th. The Indians were aware of army movements, and the entire huge village packed up and moved on that late afternoon, the day after the initial contact with Custer's forces, as Terry and Gibbon approached. By the time Terry and Gibbon arrived on the 27th, the Indians were gone.

Gibbon's first-hand account of those days, only one year after they happened, is most valuable for its immediacy and for the fact that it tells the story from the perspective of the relief column arriving first on the scene. Like other soldier accounts, it brings the reader to a time and place with a freshness that more analytical writings often cannot capture.

The handsome Gibbons (1827-1896) was a distinguished veteran of the Mexican-American and Civil Wars, as well as a West Point instructor. He led the famous Iron Brigade at the Battle of Antietam, where he had to take time away from command to temporarily man an artillery piece. He was wounded at Fredericksburg and again during Pickett's Charge at Gettysburg. He remained in the regular army and after the events described in this book, he was wounded in a fight with the Nez Perce in 1877. As commander of the Department of the Columbia, he placed

Seattle, Washington, under martial law during the anti-Chinese riots of 1886. Gibbon was a prolific writer of articles and penned books about his Civil War and Indian Wars experiences. He died in Baltimore, MD. and is buried at Arlington National Cemetery.

*And yes, we know that is Gall and not Sitting Bull on the cover. We find Gall more interesting in many ways.

BIG BYTE BOOKS

LAST SUMMER'S EXPEDITION

AGAINST THE SIOUX AND ITS GREAT CATASTROPHE.

IN the old geographies of the country an immense tract was left blank except for the words, printed across it in large letters, "*The Great American Desert*." Through a portion of this country I propose to take my readers in the present paper.

The Great Missouri River, heading in the heart of the Rocky Mountains, at about the intersection of the forty-fourth parallel with the one hundred and eleventh degree of west longitude, flows directly north for nearly four degrees, then turning to the eastward continues in that direction for about eight degrees more, and then after its junction with the waters of the Yellowstone at old Fort **Union**, near Fort Buford, doubles on its course and flows southeastwardly for hundreds of miles towards its union with the Mississippi. The northern portion of this great bend of the Missouri River was the scene of events during the spring and summer of the Centennial year, in a search for General Sitting Bull and the hostile[1] bands associated with him, some of which we will describe.

[1]Though the tribes were roaming on unceded lands given to them as hunting grounds by treaty, they had been notified early in 1876 that any bands off the reservation would be designated hostile.

With its head waters only a few miles to the south and east of those of the Missouri, the Yellowstone River also flows directly north for over a hundred miles, passing through the National Park and then turning to the eastward pursues its northeastwardly course for nearly five hundred miles to its junction with the Missouri at Fort Buford. Where it turns to the eastward the Yellowstone is only about twenty miles from Fort Ellis, at the head of the Gallatin Valley; and a few miles lower down it receives the waters of Shields's River, the only **northern** tributary it has throughout its whole course. From the **south** it receives numerous streams, heading in the mountain ranges far to the southward. The largest of these are Clarke's Fork, the Big Horn, Tongue, and Powder Rivers, all streams named by the Lewis and Clarke expedition of 1806. The largest of them all, the Big Horn, runs for several hundred miles directly north, and joins the Yellowstone at a distance of over two hundred miles from Fort Ellis, and furnishes about as much water as the main Yellowstone. It drains an immense area of country, and has numerous tributaries from the east and west. About forty miles from its mouth, it receives from the southeast the waters of the Little Big Horn, around whose name mournful memories will linger for many years to come.

On the Big Horn, seventy-five miles from its mouth, are the ruins of old Fort C. F. Smith, and eighty miles to the southeast those of Fort Phil. Kearny, the scene of the Fetterman massacre in 1866, the perpetrators being the same tribe which ten years later made a spot on the Little Big Horn, not a hundred miles away, mournfully notorious by the slaughter of the gallant Custer and his three hundred men.[2] A few miles below the mouth of the Big Horn and on the left bank of the Yellowstone, stands, or stood, Fort Pease, named after a former agent of the friendly Crows, on whose reservation, extending south of the Yellowstone and far to the eastward of the Big Horn, General Custer's battle took place on the 25th of June. Fort Pease is not, and never was, a military post It was established as a trading and "wolfing" station, was formed of little log huts connected by a line of stockade, and was" occupied by a party of hunters and trappers, whose principal occupation consisted in collecting furs from the numerous wild animals inhabiting the country. The most valuable of these are derived from the wolves, which exist there in great numbers, and those who collect the skins are known in the western country as "wolfers." The skins are most valuable in the winter season when the fur is heavy and soft, and the method of securing them cruel in the extreme. During the severe weather of winter when the ground is covered with snow the wolves in immense numbers range over the whole country, especially at night, in search of food. The quick nose of the wolf soon discovers the location of any dead animal, and it is at once eagerly devoured by the half famished animals, whose cries bring others to the scene of the feast. The "wolfer" after slaying a deer, antelope, elk, or buffalo, removes the skin, takes such portion of the meat as he wants, and then taking from his

6

pocket a little bottle of strychnine proceeds whilst the flesh is still warm to impregnate it with the poison.

²Estimates of the dead at Little Bighorn, including soldiers, scouts, and civilians in Custer's group and with Reno and Benteen at the southern defense is from 250-265.

The next morning when he visits the scene he has only to follow the wolf-tracks in the snow for a short distance to discover the bodies of all the wolves which have participated in the feast, lying where the poor animals have expired in the most intense agony.*

*In the intervening 138 years from Gibbon's writing, wolves in this area were wiped out and then slowly re-introduced, to great controversy among wildlife advocates and ranchers.

He removes the valuable skins at his leisure, or if the weather is cold waits for a milder day to perform the skinning operation.

So violent is this poison that it is said that another animal eating of the flesh of a poisoned one rapidly falls a victim to the deadly taint, and the stomach of a poisoned wolf will retain its fatal properties for a long time to come, as many a hunter with valuable dogs has found to his cost. This active poison, strychnine, is sold in immense quantities throughout this whole western country, and is, I believe, the only one used; the more common one, arsenic, producing, as is well known, no effect upon the dog-kind. The Indians are very much prejudiced against its use, and it is said they have a superstition that where it is used on dead buffalo it destroys the grass, and drives the buffalo away. The Sioux in the vicinity of Fort Pease early testified their hostility towards the "wolfer" party, and took every occasion to waylay and kill any of them who imprudently wandered too far from the post. They even threatened the post itself with attack, and so beleaguered the little garrison in the winter of 1875 and 1876 that it was with difficulty any of them could get out for procuring the necessary food or fuel. In the early spring of 1876 their cries for help became so loud that in February a command was ordered from Fort Ellis to go to the relief of Fort Pease. Four companies of cavalry started on the 2d, made the march of over two hundred miles down the Yellowstone, crossing the river several times on the ice, and returned to Fort Ellis in less than a month with the rescued trappers, having seen no Indians on the trip.

The Sioux did not confine their hostile acts to parties, like the one at Fort Pease, immediately on the borders of their hunting ground. For several years, murdering and thieving war parties had invaded the white settlements of Montana, carrying consternation, wherever they went. Cattle were slaughtered, horses stolen, and men killed in the settlements east of Fort Ellis, in the summer of 1875, and during August of that year several soldiers, whilst hunting and fishing in the vicinity of Camp Lewis, a post established for the protection of a mail and freighting route from Helena to Carroll on the Missouri River, were killed. These depredations were all supposed to be committed by

8

men belonging to a tribe presided over by a chief called Sitting Bull, a rather notorious Sioux who prided himself greatly upon standing aloof from the whites, never going to an agency and never trading with one personally, although he was not averse to trading with the agency through others. His home camp was supposed to be on the dry fork of the Missouri, a stream which running north empties into that river just above Fort Peck (a trading post and agency for the northern Indian. These war parties from his camp, operating during the summer season, would pass over vast distances on their fleet little ponies, commit their depredations, and be off hundreds of miles away before anybody but the poor victims would know anything about it.

But Montana was not the only region which suffered from these depredations. Similar transactions were taking place to the southward along the northern borders of Wyoming and Nebraska, and in the Black Hills (a region guaranteed by solemn treaty to the Indians), the "irrepressible conflict" between barbarism and the invading gold-seekers was carried on, and, as may be imagined, did not tend to bring about peaceful relations between the government and the Sioux nation. At length the government, having through its agents **starved** many of the Indians into leaving the agencies in order to get food, ordered them all back there in the depth of winter at the penalty of being proceeded against by the military, and early in March the troops took the field from the south, struck Crazy Horse's camp on Powder River, and returned.

On the very day of this occurrence (17th), five companies of infantry left Fort Shaw, and, in the midst of snow and mud, commenced their march of one hundred and eighty-three miles for Fort Ellis, whilst another company from Camp Baker dug its way through the deep snowdrifts of a mountain range, and proceeded towards the same point. These troops reached Fort Ellis in the latter part of March, probably the most inclement month of the year, and, in the midst of heavy storms of wet snow and sleet, and over roads which were simply horrible, were pushed across the divide which separates that post from the waters of the Yellowstone, under the supposition that they were moving to co-operate with General Crook's column from the south. On the 1st of April, the four companies of the Second Cavalry left Fort Ellis to follow the same road, and overtake the infantry. It proved anything but an April day. The steep and rocky road was intersected in places by streams and marshy spots where our heavily loaded wagons sunk to the hub, and on the 3d a furious storm of wind and drifting snow assailed us, so that it was midnight on the 4th before the train reached Shields's River, a distance of twenty-eight miles. This was slow progress, indeed, if we wished to co-operate with General Crook's column, the account of whose fight, some four hundred miles away, had just been received by telegraph.

The military was started out to punish and bring to subjection the hostile bands which were defying the government. These were known to be not numerous, and they were, during the summer months, in the habit of roaming at will over the vast uninhabited region I have described in the great bend of the Missouri River, hunting the buffalo, laying up their supplies of skins and meat for the winter, and varying their operations by sending out small war parties to raid upon the white settlements, or fighting the Crows, against whom they were at deadly enmity. If these were all the troops had to contend with it was natural to suppose that the moment General Crook commenced to press them from the south, these bands would move north, and, if not interfered with, would, if the pressure continued, cross the Yellowstone, and perhaps even the Missouri. Hence the necessity for other columns of troops with which to strike these moving bands on the march, or interfere to prevent their crossing to the north of the Yellowstone. For this purpose two columns moved, one from the east the other from the west, and marched towards each other. But two weeks before the Montana column started from Fort Ellis, General Crook had struck his blow, and hence the necessity for pushing forward down the Yellowstone as rapidly as possible, for the Indians, if moving north, would succeed in getting across that stream before the yearly spring rise, and before either the eastern or western column could interfere.

The original intention was to move the Montana column directly on Fort C. F. Smith by what was called the Bogeman wagon-road, then to cross the Big Horn River and move eastward, with the expectation of striking any hostile camps which might be located in that vast region watered by the Little Big Horn, Tongue, and Rosebud, but, on the receipt of the news of General Crook's fight, it was deemed advisable to move this column directly down the Yellowstone, and to keep it north instead of south of that river. This rendered necessary a change of our depot of supplies from the new Crow agency on the Stillwater, one hundred miles from Fort Ellis, to the north side of the Yellowstone River. For, in a few weeks that stream would be entirely impassable from the melting of the spring snows. A train with a month's supply of forage and rations had already been forwarded to the Crow agency. The troops found no difficulty in fording the Yellowstone River, and on the 7th the cavalry overtook the infantry in camp on the Yellowstone above the mouth of the Stillwater, where the whole command was luxuriating on the delicious trout caught in the greatest quantity from the clear and almost ice-cold waters of the Yellowstone.

I had in the morning sent forward a courier to the agency, calling a council with the Crows with a view to obtaining some of them to accompany the troops as scouts, and had requested Mitch Bowyer,[3] a noted guide and interpreter, to meet me that night in my ,camp. This man I had never seen, but he had served with troops before, and bore the reputation of being, next to the celebrated Jim Bridger, the best guide in the country. Whilst seated in my tent, the next morning, a man with the face of an Indian and the dress of a white man approached the door, and almost without saying anything seated himself on the ground, and it was some moments before I understood that my visitor was the expected guide. He was a diffident, low-spoken man, who uttered his words in a hesitating way, as if uncertain what he was going to say. He brought the news that the Crows were waiting to see me, and mounting my I horse I was with a small party soon on the road to the agency, which we reached after a disagreeable ride of eighteen miles through a severe storm of wet snow. The agency, Situated amidst bleak and barren hills, was surrounded by the teepies of some three thousand Crows, scattered in family groups all over the little valley of Rosebud Creek, a branch of the Stillwater.

[3]Bowyer (also spelled Bouyer or Boyer) was a mixed-heritage (Sioux-French) scout who reportedly challenged Custer about there being too many Indians in the Little Big Horn Valley for the number of troops Custer was leading against them.

The next day, Sunday, the chiefs assembled in council to hear my "talk" and the proposition to furnish us scouts. Somewhat to my surprise the proposition did not appear to be favorably received, and when an Indian does not want to do a thing he resembles a white man a good deal, and has a thousand and one excellent reasons why he should not do it. They listened in silence to the interpreter as he translated, or ***appeared*** to translate, what I said. For when he came to translate their answer to me he strung his English words together in such a fearfully incongruous way as made me tremble at the idea that my eloquent appeal to the chiefs had been murdered in the Crow tongue, as he was murdering the English in conveying to me their answer.

These Indian interpreters are a peculiar institution. As a class, they are an interesting study, and will bear generally a good deal of watching. A white man, usually a renegade from civil society, takes up his abode with a tribe of Indians, adopts their mode of life, takes unto himself a squaw, picks up gradually enough of their signs and words to make himself understood, and when the Indians come in contact with the whites becomes, in the absence of any other means of communication, an "interpreter." He may not understand the English language, or be able to put together a single intelligible sentence, and it does not mend the matter much if he happens to be a French Canadian, for then broken French, broken English, and broken Indian are mixed up in a hodge-podge which defies all understanding and makes the listener sometimes give up in despair. I suspect many an Indian commissioner would stand aghast could he have ***literally*** translated to him the perfect jumble of words in which the "interpreter" had conveyed his eloquent and carefully prepared speech to the ears of his red audience. For this reason it is a matter of some importance in communicating with Indians to make use of the plainest language and the shortest sentences, and even then you are by no means sure that anything like what you intended is conveyed to your listeners, especially if what you say does not happen to meet the peculiar views or interests of the one who, for the want of a better term, is called an "interpreter." The one who officiated on this occasion appeared to try to be making up by gesticulations and a loud voice for any defects in his knowledge of language. I believe he did finally succeed in conveying to the Indians the information that we wanted twenty-five of their young active warriors to accompany us to the field and serve as the *"eyes"* of the expedition, in spying out the country and giving us information regarding the location of the Sioux camps.

The talk was received in silence, followed by a very earnest discussion amongst themselves, after which two of the principal chiefs, Iron Bull and Blackfoot, replied to the effect that if the young men wanted to go they could go, but that if they did not want to go they (the chiefs) could not make them; that they were friends to the white man and desired to remain at peace with him; appealed to the Almighty (the interpreter called him *Godalamity*) as to the sincerity of what they said, and ended with what I fear is a very common appeal now amongst Indians, for more flour and beef than was issued to them. But one single man seemed to talk in favor of going to war, but they asked time to talk about it amongst themselves, for such weighty matters are never decided in a hurry, and have to be discussed with due deliberation and the appropriate amount of smoke. So the council broke up without any definite conclusion being reached, and I began to think we should have to enter the Sioux country blindfolded. I soon discovered, however, that only the "old fogies" had spoken in council, and that as soon as "Young America" had a chance to be heard in the camps our chance for obtaining scouts improved, and the next morning the whole number required came forward and were sworn into the United States service. This ceremony was peculiar. We wished to bind them to their contract in some way, and in casting round for a method were informed that the Crow's way to take an oath was to **touch with his finger the point of a knife.** After this solemn proceeding if he failed to stand up to his pledges he was a disgraced man; but what was far more likely to keep him faithful was the belief that a violation of the oath laid him open to direful calamities in the way of disease and misfortune, not only to himself, but to all the members of his family! All the volunteers were paraded, and an officer presented to each in succession a hunting knife, on the point of which each one gravely placed the tip of his forefinger and the deed was done. They thus became United States soldiers for three months, and were to receive soldier's pay, rations, and clothing. After all had gone through the ceremony, one of them took the knife and gravely presented the point of it to me. When asked why he wished to swear me, he said he wished to bind me to do what **they** said; but I told them I could not do that, for the obligation to obey was on their side alone.

The officer who swore them in offered to swear that he would see they got all the pay, rations, etc., they were entitled to, and as all they wanted apparently was some kind of a mutual obligation, they readily consented to this, and the officer solemnly touched the point of the knife.

I will not burden my readers with the long list of the long names of the twenty-five warriors who thus engaged to join us in our campaign against the Sioux, but will mention simply the names of several who afterwards became noted amongst us.

Ee-suh-see-ush, whose English name was "Show-his-Face," was an old man, who went along with no idea of engaging in the labors of war, but accompanied the party simply to give it character, and bestow upon the younger members the benefit of his advice. He was early looked upon as what in Western phraseology is called a "coffee-cooler," a fellow who loafs around the camp-fire, and whose principal occupation consists in cooling *and* drinking coffee from a tincup. From his supposed resemblance to a venerable senator from the State of Pennsylvania he soon became known in the camp as "The Senator."

Iss-too-sah-shee-dah, Half-yellow-Face, was a large, fine-looking Indian, who afterwards became a great favorite with us, and was one of the six Crows who accompanied the Seventh Cavalry and was present with it in its fight on the 25th of June.

Mee-uah-tsee-us, White Swan, also accompanied the Seventh Cavalry, and was badly wounded in the battle.

Shuh-shee-ahsh, Curly Hair, was quite a young man and became noted afterwards as the one single person who, of all those taken into action under the immediate command of General Custer, made his escape.

On the 10th our wagon train arrived from the camp, our supplies were loaded up and ready to start the next morning for the depot to be established on the north bank of the Yellowstone. That night a furious storm of wind and snow raged, and we opened our eyes to find the ground covered with two feet of snow and rapidly deepening. To remain stationary, however, was simply to contemplate the possibility of being snowed up in the mountains for a week, perhaps longer. As soon, therefore, as the harness could be dug out of the snow, and the teams hitched up we started to plough through the deep snow notwithstanding the storm, which still raged directly in our faces. As we receded from the mountains, however, the snow decreased in depth, the storm abated, and the train reached camp late at night, the only mishap being the loss of two mules drowned in crossing the Yellowstone at a ford which was quite a deep and rapid one.

All the supplies and extra baggage which we could not carry in our wagons we now prepared to leave here under charge of one of the infantry companies, and, with the remainder of the command and our heavily loaded wagons, we resumed the march down the Yellowstone. The ground was, however, very soft from the melting snow, and the teams labored slowly along. For several days we made but little progress, and only reached Baker's battle-ground, a distance of forty-three miles, on the 15th. This was the scene of an attack made by Indians in 1872 upon a body of our troops engaged in escorting the engineers of the Northern Pacific Railroad Company.

Below this, in order to avoid the rough broken ground extending for miles along the north of the river, we were obliged to cross once more to the southern bank, at a ford which was deep and rapid, and came very near proving fatal to one of our officers. His horse yielding to the force of the swiftly rushing current soon got out of his depth, and in an instant both he and his rider disappeared beneath the surface of the water. Soon the horse's head came up and then the rider's; but to the horror of the lookers-on the horse seemed to be utterly incapable of swimming, and engaged in frantic struggles, without aim or object, in the course of which he nearly fell over backwards on his rider. The current fortunately, as it swept them along, carried them close enough to the river-bank to strike bottom, when horse and rider, the latter still clinging to the bridle, but chilled with the ice-cold water, were pulled ashore.

On the south side of the river there is no longer any road, and we have to make our way as best we can through the thick heavy sage brush of the valley to Prior's Creek, which we find a deep rushing torrent of muddy snow-water, with high banks. Crossing this delays us so long that the day is far towards its close when we go into camp, chafing at having made only seven miles.

The next day brought us to the far-famed Pompey's Pillar, almost under the shadow of which we camped. It is an irregular mass of sandstone, rising several hundred feet above the level of the valley on the south side of the river, and evidently belonged originally to a corresponding bluff on the opposite side of the river, from which it has been separated by the wearing away of the intervening rock. The account of Lewis and Clarke mentions that a fine view of the surrounding country was had from the top of Pompey's Pillar, which was ascended by Captain Clarke for that purpose the day the expedition passed the pillar, which is stated in their journal to have been, the 25th of July, 1806. I climbed up the not very steep ascent on the eastern side, and whilst resting on one of the ledges read over the names, which, in travellers' fashion, were roughly scribbled over the face of the soft sandstone, until I came to this:

Wm Clarke

July 25th 1806

My first thought was that some later visitor had amused himself by inscribing the great explorer's name on this landmark; but an examination of the more recent inscriptions showed them all to be light-colored, whilst the lines of this one were of the same tint as the face of the brown sandstone upon which the writing was placed, and I remained satisfied that I stood face to face with Captain Clarke's name inscribed nearly seventy years before. I continued the ascent, pondering over the different circumstances surrounding me in this Centennial year of the country, and those under which Captain Clarke climbed up when the nation was but thirty-one years old, and this whole region one vast wilderness. On reaching the top I found myself standing upon a grass-grown mound surrounded on three sides by a sheer precipice of perpendicular rock, down which it made one's head swim to look. To the north, across the beautiful clear river, rose a mass of rough broken hills, whilst to the south and west extended the broad flat plain of the river bottom, bordered on the north by a curved line of timber which marked the course of the river, and to the south by a range of bluffs which, opening in one place to allow the passage of Fly Creek, permitted the eye to range far up its little valley towards the mouth of the Little Big Horn River, afterwards to play so prominent a part in the history of our campaign.

With a view to the examination of that region the command laid over here one day, and scouts were sent off in that direction. They returned without having seen any sign of Indians, but reported that the whole valley of the Big Horn was black with countless herds of buffalo quietly feeding, the best of signs that no Indians are close about, and yet the best in the world that they are not very far away; for the buffalo herd is the natural **commissary** of the Indians on the plains, and they constantly follow this moving depot of supplies. When they commence to hunt them, the buffalo immediately about the hunting-grounds stampede and run for miles, pushing the rest of the herd before them. Hence, if the buffalo are quietly feeding you may be sure there is no pressure from behind, and no Indians near. But if on the contrary the herd is found to be moving, you may look out for Indians, as surely as you look for cars behind an approaching locomotive.

Ordinarily on reaching camp both officers and men are so tired out with the march that as soon as the evening meal is finished, and the night guard posted, all are ready to seek that sleep, the want of which tells fearfully upon the physical forces the next day, and usually by nine o'clock, frequently earlier, the whole camp except the sentinels are wrapped in deep slumber, which is enjoyed securely, with the knowledge that several pairs of eyes are peering out into the darkness and the same number of pairs of ears eagerly on the alert to detect the approach of any prowling Indians who may be seeking an opportunity to steal our animals. But after a day's rest the powers are recuperated, groups are formed around the blazing camp-fires, and the still night re-echoes with songs sung in full chorus. Such an evening was spent under the tall cottonwoods of our camp at Pompey's Pillar, and long after the campfires were out and everything was still, the thoughts of many of us wandered off towards those "true loves," who, in the words of the ringing chorus, still echoing in our ears, were, so far as communicating with them was concerned,

"Playing the grand in a distant land,

Ten thousand miles away."

During the next day's march the bluffs on both sides abutted so closely on the river as to force us to ford the stream twice within a distance of two miles, and now haste becomes all the more necessary, for the river is evidently rising, and we must make our last crossing so as to be on the north side before it becomes impassable. Our guide, Mitch Bowyer, is of inestimable value now, for he rides forward to search for a crossing, and is an indefatigable worker, riding his hardy little pony into the ice-cold water sometimes to a swimming depth, testing the crossings where anybody thinks there is a chance to get our wagons over. At last the shallowest point is found, and although deeper than is comfortable we must take to the water, for we cannot afford to wait another day. A company of cavalry, with its old soldier captain at its head, mounted on his old and long-tried favorite, "Dick," enters the ford, stringing out in a long curved line behind as brave old "Dick" breasts the rushing and rapidly deepening stream. Higher and higher rises the water, and just as we begin to think some of the smaller horses will have to swim, "Dick's" shoulder commences to emerge, and the worst is passed. Now the wagons, covered with infantrymen, start in, and as they approach the deepest part some of the smaller mules barely have their backs above the water, but still they struggle on, seeming to understand as well as their drivers that when crossing a river is no time "to swap horses." Suddenly down goes the forepart of one of the wagons, and for a moment it is a matter of doubt whether a wheel is broken or is in a hole. The mules struggle and plunge, fall down and get up again, the drivers, outsiders, and men shout out their loudest yells to encourage the frantic animals, and at last the long line of wagons reaches the opposite shore, water pouring from every crack of the wagon-bodies, which makes us hope that the bottom layer of each load is bacon rather than "hardtack" and bedding. Our dripping teams are given a short rest, mounted officers and men pour the water from their boots, and we all feel relieved that we are on the right bank of the river at last. A few miles further, and from the top of the bluffs bordering the valley of the Yellowstone we catch sight of the walls of Fort Pease, still standing, with a little United States flag fluttering in the breeze.

The next day a courier arrived from Camp Supply, bringing an important dispatch from department headquarters. It had reached Camp Supply just after the departure of two couriers with our mail, and an energetic young son of one of our officers started with it, accompanied by a single soldier, to ride a hundred miles and bring it to me. He followed our trail, saw nothing of the other couriers, crossed, with great difficulty, the river at our last ford, and reached our camp in safety. The dispatch was dated at St. Paul on the 15th (six days before), and informed me that General Crook would not be prepared to take the field before the middle of May, that the third column had not yet started, and directed that I proceed no farther than the mouth of the Big Horn unless sure of striking a successful blow. Our camp was, therefore, moved down to Fort Pease, and for three weeks we were engaged in what to a soldier is the hardest of all duties—*waiting.*

Advantage was taken of this delay to send back our wagon train under charge of a company, to bring up the rest of our supplies, and to thoroughly examine the valleys of Little and Big Horn in the direction of old Fort C. F. Smith. This latter was accomplished by a scouting party of two companies of cavalry, which left us on the 24th and returned on the 1st of May, having seen no signs of Indians during the trip.

On the 30th, some of our Indian scouts returned from the Rosebud, reporting that country free from any signs of Indians, and it began to look as if they had all fled to the agencies. Our Crow scouts are kept constantly on the alert, some of them being out every day, early and late. They appear to be of a nervous, excitable temperament, and some of them came running in one day to announce the approach of a party of Sioux. A mounted party was at once sent out to reconnoitre, and came back with the information that the scouts had seen one of our hunting parties, and took them for Sioux.

Fort Pease is situated directly on the bank of the river, at the edge of a wide open prairie. Directly opposite, on the other side of the river, a steep rocky bluff rises up almost perpendicularly from the edge of the water, and this our scouts were in the habit of using as a lookout, crossing the river in a small boat, several of which were found at the fort when we arrived there. The 1st of May was a bright clear day, and about noon the whole camp was startled by hearing loud and continued yells from the opposite bluffs. Immediately the Crows in camp seized their arms, and started on a run for their pony herd, grazing about a mile from camp. Looking up to the top of the bluff, four Indians could be seen running in single file at the top of their speed, and uttering the most piercing screams. They looked as if about to pitch over the perpendicular bluff into the river below; but just before reaching the edge, the leader commenced circling around, followed by the others, all uttering the wildest shrieks, and then all disappeared behind a projecting point, to reappear soon after at a lower point, still on the full run. The running in a circle was the signal for "an enemy in sight" and word was sent to draw in the herd. In an incredibly short space of time the scouts had crossed the river, and came panting into camp with the information that they had seen a large war party of Sioux coming out of the valley of Tullock's Fork. As I was expecting the scouting party from Fort Smith, I suggested that it might be that; but they declared they were not white men, did not move like them, and were far too numerous to be our scouting party, and altogether were so positive and confident, and moreover apparently so hurt that I should think they could confound white men and Sioux, that I began to have serious misgivings in regard to the safety of our two little companies of cavalry, and to imagine that they had met with serious disaster, and the victorious Sioux were now coming in to pay their respects to us. Hence I was very much relieved when, a few hours later, our friends, dripping from the deep ford of the Yellowstone, rode into camp and reported the result of their scout. The Crows looked crestfallen at the idea of their false cry of "the wolf," but were soon to learn by sad experience that the "wolf" was even closer than they thought, for the very next day a heavy windstorm set in, and all that night the camp and vicinity were swept with driving clouds of dust, through which objects could be seen only at a few paces' distance. Just such a night do Indians select for their thieving expeditions, and early the next morning one of our white scouts came into camp and exhibited, with a rueful countenance, a picket-pin with two bits of rope cut off close to the pin-head. The night before, that picket-pin had been driven into the ground a hundred yards outside of our line of camp sentinels, the bits of rope were thin lariats, and at their opposite extremities were tied to graze two of his own animals, a horse and a mule. Now, all of his property that remained was this picket-pin and the cleanly severed ends of his lariats. All our own animals were inside the line of sentinels, as his two should have been. We had never been able to bring our Crows sufficiently under military control to induce them to keep their ponies in camp at night, and they were permitted to roam at large night and day in search of subsistence. The lonely picket-pin demonstrated beyond doubt that "the wolf" had come, and that the thieving Sioux had paid our camp a visit. It did not take long to make the discovery that the whole pony herd of the Crows, some thirty in number, had, alas, disappeared, and the scene which followed was absurd in the extreme. The Crows assembled at their camp and *cried* like children whose toys had been broken. There is nothing unnatural in a crying child, and the manly grief of a broken heart excites one's sympathy, but to see a parcel of great big Indians standing together and blubbering like babies, with great tears streaming down their swarthy faces because they had lost their horses, struck every one as supremely ridiculous. Scouting parties were sent out, the trail of the marauders discovered leading down the river, and signs found which left no doubt of their being Sioux.

On the 8th our train, with the two companies, arrived from Camp Supply, and the whole command being now together, with wagons enough to carry all our stores, I decided to move farther down the river. There were evidently nothing more than small war parties about us, and my reiterated instructions were to guard as much as possible against the Indians crossing the Yellowstone to go north. The principal crossing-places were lower down near the mouth of Rosebud River, and on this side. We moved on the 10th, but were delayed by bad roads made worse by a furious rainstorm, and on the fifth day had made only fifty-two miles to a camp a short distance above the mouth of the Rosebud. Here we were visited by a heavy hail and rainstorm, which stampeded our animals, flooded our camp, and rendered the surrounding country impassable for wagons. Both sides of the river were kept well scouted, and on the 17th one of our party reported the presence on Tongue River, some thirty-five miles distant, of an Indian camp. The Yellowstone was now a raging torrent of muddy water; but we had, on leaving Fort Pease, brought along several small boats found there, and with the assistance of these it was determined to throw a force across the river, and by a night march, surprise the camp on Tongue River. Pack saddles were now got out, extra ammunition and rations issued, and preparations made to cross the river with the whole force except one company, which was left at our camp in charge of the train. The crossing-place selected was about a mile above the camp. The boats were pulled up there and used to cross over the men, saddles, etc., of a company. The horses of the company were then brought down to the shore and an attempt made to drive them into the water. They resisted stoutly; but a few finally entered the water, which was cold and rapid. But no sooner did they lose their footing and commence to swim than, turning round, they returned to our shore, followed by the few which had ventured in after them. Again and again were they forced to the water's edge, but with the same result, and finally the whole of them broke from the men around them and stampeded back to camp. Several hours were consumed in these fruitless efforts, and then a different plan was tried. One of the oldest horses was selected, and to his tail was firmly tied the halter of another; to the tail of this one another, and so on till a long line of half a dozen were tied together. A rope attached to the leader was now taken into the boat manned by rowers and the boat pulled out from shore. The leader quietly followed, dragging his trail behind him, whilst the loose horses, seeing so many going in, followed in a body, urged on by the shouting men. Soon the deep water was reached and the leader began to swim, followed in fine style by the others, and everything was looking favorable for the passage of the horses at last, when suddenly the whole scene changed and one of the most indescribable confusion followed. From some cause or other the boats became unmanageable in the swift current, and instead of keeping on a straight course with a taut rope stretching to the leading horse, it floated for a moment at the mercy of the current, the rope became slack, the rear horses continued to swim forward, the third or fourth horse got across the line in front of the leader, and in an instant the water was filled with a tangled mass of frantic animals struggling for life. Most of the hitching halters held, and the longer the poor creatures struggled the worse entangled they became. Some soon became exhausted and sunk beneath the ice-cold muddy torrent; some few continued across and landed on the other shore, but most of them returned, whilst one powerful beast waded back, pulling after him a comrade which had fallen exhausted and died in water so shallow that only about one-half his body was covered. Four horses were drowned outright, and the rest so frightened that they could not be again made to approach the water. It was now late in the afternoon, the attempt to cross the river was abandoned, the few men and horses thrown across were brought back and the troops returned to camp. We were now, perforce, confined in our operations to the north side of the river, up and down which mounted parties were constantly kept on the move, and occasionally two or three of the Crows would cross and reconnoitre the south side, or start on horse-stealing expeditions; but in each case they returned unsuccessful and disappointed.

One day whilst seated in my tent I heard the distant cry of a wolf. Wondering at the bark of a cayote in broad daylight, my attention was attracted by a great commotion amongst the Crows, several of whom with their guns started on the run for the river-bank, repeating the wolf-like cry. It was answered from across the river, and jumping into one of the boats they soon returned with two of their number, who had gone off on a horse-stealing expedition, and now, having been unsuccessful, were coming back, and took this way of informing their friends of the fact

On the 18th two companies of cavalry were started on a scout to the mouth of Tongue River, and two days afterwards the Crows reported a heavy force of Indians moving towards the mouth of the Rosebud, evidently with the design of crossing the Yellowstone. Leaving one company of infantry in charge of the camp, the remainder of the command was pushed hastily down the river, and bivouacked for the night just below the mouth of the

Rosebud. No Indians, however, were seen, nor any indications of a projected crossing, and the next day the remainder of the camp was brought down to the new position, and the two companies from below joined us. They had gone down as far as the mouth of Tongue River, had seen a party of about fifty Indians trying evidently to get across to our side, and not having themselves been seen, had laid in wait for them several hours. But the Indians after several attempts to cross, had evidently given it up, and proceeded up the river on the other side. On leaving, however, they had concealed their extra ponies in the timber, and with the idea that they had left no guard to look after them, Mitch Bowyer and one of the Crows with the scouting party conceived a bold attempt to capture these ponies. Stripping, and without a weapon of any kind, they swam the Yellowstone, and crept through the timber to within sight of the grazing animals, which they found under charge of two Indian boys. To get to them they were obliged to pass an open space, and no sooner did their naked forms leave the shelter of the timber than they were perceived by the watchful boys, who with loud shouts hurried the band of ponies off into the hills beyond their reach, and Mitch and his companion had nothing to do but to swim back to their own side of the river.

We had in the command a number of fine shots, and permission was constantly given these men to hunt, and by them the country in the vicinity of our camps and line of march was kept very well scouted. One of these parties reported on the 22d that they had been fired upon by Indians in the hills that day, but they were evidently not in great force, for the scouting parties sent out discovered but few pony tracks, and saw no Indians. The next morning early the pickets reported firing in the hills. Several hunting parties were out, but the firing being continued, and a number of horsemen making their appearance on the bluff about three miles from camp, two companies of cavalry were at once sent out in that direction, and it was then for the first time discovered that two men belonging to one of these companies and a citizen teamster were absent from camp without authority. Why they should go without permission when all they had to do was to ask for it, I could not imagine, and it is a singular fact that of all the parties out that morning this one of three was the only one to encounter Indians. The cavalry started at once for the point where the horsemen had been seen to disappear on the bluffs. On reaching the foot-hills the party found itself in the midst of a succession of knolls rising higher and higher, and forming a number of narrow valleys. The men appear to have entered one of these blindly without taking any precaution in the way of a lookout. They were doubtless watched from the high ground, and parties of Indians posted out of sight behind the hills on each side permitted the three hunters to advance until surrounded on all sides, and then making their appearance, delivered their fire from several directions upon the doomed men. The bodies were found stripped, shot in several places and horribly mutilated, with heads beaten in, and one of the men had two knives, taken from the bodies of his dead comrades, driven into the sides of his head. The knife of the third man was afterwards recognized and picked up on Custer's battle-field. When the cavalry reached the top of the bluffs, not an Indian was to be seen. The trail was followed for some miles, but the only thing seen of the party was a single horseman rapidly disappearing on a distant hill. The bodies were brought into camp and laid side by side to rest under a large cottonwood tree, upon the trunk of which, after removing the bark an appropriate inscription was placed, and heavy logs piled up over the grave to guard against the action of wolves. As the scouting party came into camp about sundown, quite a number of heads appeared cautiously above a distant hill on the other side of the river, and from this time forth our camp was doubtless very carefully watched.

We had now been out nearly two months, and our supplies were becoming short. I had sent back to Fort Ellis for more supplies, and had information that they were on the road. For the double purpose of escorting this train in, and taking back a number of surplus contractors' wagons, two companies left our camp in charge of a train the very morning of the murders (23d), and we now had nothing to do but to await the arrival of our supplies, keeping the river above and below well scouted by parties of cavalry. I had received dispatches from General Terry that he expected to reach the Yellowstone at the mouth of the Glendive Creek about the 28th, and on the 27th I called for volunteers to carry a dispatch down the river by boat. Two men who afterwards became quite noted for a deed of great daring, offered their services for the trip. Their names were Evans and Stewart, both soldiers, belonging to Captain Clifford's company of the Seventh Infantry. They were accompanied by a white scout, named Williamson, and just at dark, with muffled oars, they got into their frail bark and noiselessly dropped down the stream on their perilous and uncertain voyage, many of their comrades assembling on the bank to see them off. The very next morning I received by boat from Fort Ellis an important dispatch from department headquarters. It informed me that General Terry had left Fort Lincoln on the morning of the 15th; that he had received information that the hostiles were concentrated on the Little Missouri, and between that and the Powder River; that he anticipated opposition between the Missouri River and the Yellowstone, and directed me to march at once to a point on the Yellowstone opposite Stanley's stockade, to cross the river, if possible, and advance to meet him on Stanley's trail, and to use one of the steamers which I would probably find there for crossing my command. The point designated was some one hundred and fifty miles from where we then were. A speedy movement was evidently expected, and yet with the region about us infested with hostile Indians, how could we leave the large train of supplies now on the road to follow us with its escort of one small company of infantry? All our wagons were at once unloaded, and the next morning under charge of two companies started back to lighten the supply train, and hurry it forward as fast as possible. Notwithstanding a furious *snow*-storm, which raged all day on the 1st of June, our train made good time, and reached camp on the 4th, so that the command was now once more together, and its supplies with it. The morning of the 5th found us on our way down the river once more, every one eager to push forward and join the Lincoln column. But we were now entering upon a comparatively unknown region, and on the second day encountered a single hill which required four hours and a great deal of hard work to get our train up, and, on the third, after a march of twenty-one and a half miles, had made only forty-one miles. Mitch Bowyer informed us that the roads passed over heretofore were good compared with those we should have in the next few days, when we should be compelled to enter a terrible section of the *"Mauvaise terres."*

On the morning of the 8th, our scouts reported Indians in front, and, later on, two who had followed on the trail of two horsemen brought in a package which told us a tale words could not have made plainer. The package consisted of a small sack containing a number of army cartridges, some small round crackers, such as are kept for sale in the subsistence department, and a piece of *cheese*. The last-named article Indians seldom, if ever, use, and would never carry on a trip, so that the contents of this little sack told us as plainly as if the news had been received in a letter that General Terry was close by, and was trying to communicate with us by couriers, and that the couriers were white men.

We camped that night in the open prairie on the bank of the Yellowstone, and about two o'clock in the morning, I was waked out of a sound sleep by loud shouts. Jumping up, I reached the picket-line in time to receive a white man and an Indian, who brought dispatches from General Terry at the mouth of the Powder River. He had reached that stream without encountering any Indians, and invited me to meet him coming up the river on the steamer *Far West* the next morning. I learned too that the sack and its contents picked up by our scouts the day before had been correctly interpreted. It had been dropped by one of two white men who had been sent to communicate with us. They had seen from a distance our Crow scouts, had taken them for Sioux, and had fled back to report the country filled with hostiles, and lose a reward of two hundred dollars which had been promised them if they got through to me with their dispatches, dropping in their flight the articles which were picked up the day after by my scouts, who had never even seen the men who dropped them.

The morning of the 9th I proceeded down the valley with a company of cavalry, and soon had a specimen of the bad lands referred to by Mitch Bowyer as existing in the vicinity of Powder River, north of the Yellowstone. We climbed up an almost inaccessible mountain, being several times obliged to dismount and lead our horses, and on reaching the top had a fine view of the valley of the Yellowstone beyond far down in the direction of Powder River. The muddy rapid stream wound around the foot of the mountain almost directly beneath us, and through the fringe of timber on its banks little puffs of white steam rose up and revealed the presence of a steamer slowly making her way up against the strong current. It was the most civilized scene we had witnessed for more than two months, and as the deep hoarse voice of the steam-whistle broke upon the still morning air, the top of what we afterwards named "Steamboat Point" resounded with a loud cheer of welcome from our little party. Following a buffalo trail down the steep side of the Point we were soon on board the steamer and on our way back to camp, where the men flocked down to the bank to welcome the second steamer which had ever been so far up the waters of the Yellowstone.

The existence of any large camps of hostile Indians in this region was now more than ever a matter of doubt; for General Terry had discovered no trace of any on his march from Fort Lincoln to the Powder River, which he had reached at a point twenty-five miles above its mouth. He informed me that he had heard nothing from General Crook, and intended on his return to Powder River to send a cavalry command on a scout up that river and across it west to the Tongue and Rosebud. If no Indians should be discovered then the only remaining chance would be higher up the Yellowstone, where from my observation there must be some Indians, and if General Crook should strike them from the south, it would be all the more necessary for us to guard the line of the river and prevent any escape to the northward. He therefore instructed me to retrace my steps and await his arrival at the mouth of the Rosebud, and as dispatch was now of more importance than ever I agreed to start the cavalry part of my command that afternoon. The General had no guide at his disposal acquainted with the country south of the Yellowstone, and I suggested that he take Mitch Bowyer, who had proved so valuable to us, and was I knew well acquainted with that country. Mitch, always ready and willing, assented at once, and as soon as he and his horse were on board the steamer started down the river, and preparations were at once made to commence the march back. Before, however, the cavalry was ready to move one of those terrific rain-storms, of which we had had so many, set in. The whole alkali flat around us became one immense quagmire, and a gulch back of our camp, which was dry when we came, was soon a torrent ten or twelve feet deep. This rendered any movement out of the question until the afternoon of the next day, when the cavalry succeeded only in making a few miles, and the next day (11th) were overtaken by the infantry, having been delayed to build a road and pull up a very steep hill, it being impossible to follow the road used coming down on account of Sunday Creek being impassable from high water. All the bridges built and crossings cut during the trip down were found washed away by the heavy rains, and the low grounds were filled with driftwood brought down from the hills through the gulches, which, except during heavy rains, are entirely deprived of water.

Finally, the whole command was reunited on the 14th at the mouth of the Rosebud, where we waited for the arrival of General Terry, keeping in the meantime the country well scouted up and down the river. Four days afterwards (18th) a party of horsemen was reported by our scouts as coming down the Rosebud, and riding to a point about three miles above our camp. I started a couple of Crows to swim across the river, then higher and more rapid than ever, with a note to General Terry. The Indians stripped and commenced their preparations for their cold swim by rubbing themselves all over with red paint. I had the curiosity to inquire the object of this, and was surprised to learn that it was to protect them against the attack of *alligators*. As the alligator is an animal unknown to the waters of this region, the fact referred to is a curious evidence of the southern origin of the Crows, at the same time that it shows how traditions are transmitted for long ages in a barbarous tribe. Having completed their preparations against the attack of an animal of which perhaps their progenitors long ago had a wholesome dread in more southern waters, the note to General Terry was tied in the scalplock of one of them, and the two men started on the run for a point higher up the river. There providing themselves with a log of dead wood, they plunged into the water, and singing to keep up their courage, they were swept past us down the swift current, and after a swim of nearly a mile landed safely on the other side, and were seen through our glasses to approach the party opposite. All this took time, and being curious to know who was in the party, one of our officers tied a handkerchief to a stick, and commenced waving it from side to side as a signal. It was soon answered in the same way, and before our Crows had reached the opposite bank, the army code of signals was spelling out for us the information we wanted. In this way we learned that the party was composed of six companies of the Seventh Cavalry under command of Colonel Reno, which had been on a scout up Powder River and across the Tongue to the Rosebud,[4] and had seen no Indians, though signs of camps had been discovered on the last-named stream and a large trail leading up it. Our Crows swam back to us with a note from Colonel Reno, and the poor fellows were very much exhausted when they reached us. Could we have known what had taken place only twenty-four hours before on the head waters of the very stream at whose mouth we stood, the information would have been invaluable to us, and probably have given a different shape to our whole subsequent operations. As it was, we were still groping in the dark in regard to the location of the hostile camps, and had every reason to believe that the Sioux with their women and children were solicitous only to avoid us. General Terry was understood to be at the mouth of the Tongue River, and the next morning Colonel Reno started with his command to join him. Our scouts reported seeing large fires in the direction of the Little Horn, and now every one was anxious for the arrival of General Terry, for our last chance for striking the Indians appeared to be in the direction indicated.

[4]Gibbon does not mention here that Major Reno explicitly violated his orders by going as far as the Rosebud. By doing so, however, he found evidence of large, abandoned camps. Custer was instructed by Terry to move to Reno's position and take command of both his and Reno's men [Gray, 1991].

Anticipating a move up the river, I ordered, on the 21st, three companies of infantry to proceed up the road to replace the bridges, and repair the crossings over the various streams destroyed by the recent rains. During the morning General Terry reached our camp on the "Far West." After conferring with him, the whole command was at once started up the river, and at his request I accompanied him on the steamer to meet General Custer, who was coming up on the other side with the whole of his regiment. The steamer was run up to the mouth of the Rosebud, and afterwards dropped down to a point below, where Custer had arrived in the afternoon, and gone into camp or rather bivouac. As soon as we were tied up to the bank, he came aboard, and seated in the cabin with a map before us, we discussed the proposed operations. The large trail found by Colonel Reno leading up the Rosebud and the fires seen in that direction by my scouts led to the belief that the Indians, if overtaken at all, would be found somewhere on the Little Big Horn, a favorite resort, where the grazing was good and game close by. It was therefore arranged that General Custer should start the next day with the whole of his regiment, take up the trail on the Rosebud, and follow it; that my command should march to the mouth of the Big Horn, something over sixty miles distant, be there ferried across the Yellowstone, and march from there to the valley of the Little Big Horn, and up that stream to co-operate with Custer's command. An examination of the map showed that the course of the Rosebud approaches that of the Little Big Horn nearest at a point about as far distant from where we then were as the mouth of the Big Horn was from us. Were then Custer, whose command was exclusively of cavalry, marching with pack-mules, to follow the trail directly into the valley of the Little Big Horn,, he would probably strike the Indians long before I could be anywhere in the vicinity with my command, part of which was infantry, and to prevent the escape of the Indians, which was the idea pervading the minds of all of us, it was desirable that the two commands should be as near each other as possible when they approached the supposed location of the camp. The Indians, if struck, would probably not retreat *west,* for in that direction was the formidable Big Horn, beyond which was the whole Crow nation, the deadly enemies of the Sioux. They could not go north without running into my column, nor east without doubling on their course, and exposing themselves to attack from both columns. They would, therefore, in all probability, go south; for, in addition to its being their natural and only practicable line of retreat, was the fact that in that direction lay the Big Horn range of mountains, in the fastnesses of which they would be comparatively secure, and could live on the game and wild berries which abounded there. But if, as we had good reason to expect, General Crook's column was somewhere in that direction, there was a third column against which the Indians incumbered with their families were liable to run. Hence it was agreed that Custer, instead of proceeding at once into the valley of the Little Big Horn, even should the trail lead there, should continue on up the Rosebud, get closer to the mountains, and then striking west, come down the valley of the Little Big Horn, "feeling constantly to his left," to be sure that the Indians had not already made their escape to the south and eastward. General Terry, applying a scale to the map, measured the distances, and made the calculation in miles that each command would have to travel. My command having already started, was to be at the mouth of the Big Horn prepared to cross the Yellowstone on the third day.

The scouts with Custer's regiment were entirely ignorant of the country he was to pass through. Mitch Bowyer, who knew all about it, was to go with him, and in addition, by direction of General Terry, I assigned to duty with him six of my Crow scouts who volunteered for the service. Besides this, General Terry expressed a desire that Custer should communicate with him by sending a scout down the valley of Tullock's Fork, and send him any news of importance he might have, especially as to whether or not any hostiles were on that stream. As he had no one with him suitable for this service, I engaged, by General Terry's order, a white man named Horendem,[5] who had been with my column for some time, was a good scout, and well acquainted with the country he would have to pass over.

Horendem stipulated that in case he was called upon to incur the additional risk of carrying dispatches his compensation should be increased. This was agreed to, and he accompanied General Custer's troops.

5This was George Herendeen, not Horendom.

At noon the next day, General Terry, accompanied by myself and General Brisbin, rode to the upper end of the camp to witness the departure of Custer and his fine regiment. The bugles sounded the "boots and saddles," and Custer, after starting the advance, rode up and joined us. Together we sat on our horses and witnessed the approach of the command as it threaded its way through the rank sage brush which covered the valley. First came a band of buglers sounding a march, and as they came opposite to General Terry they wheeled out of the column as at review, continuing to play as the command passed along. The regiment presented a fine appearance, and as the various companies passed us we had a good opportunity to note the number of fine horses in the ranks, many of them being part-blooded horses from Kentucky, and I was told there was not a single sore-backed horse amongst them.[6] General Custer appeared to be in good spirits, chatted freely with us, and was evidently proud of the appearance of his command. The pack mules, in a compact body, followed the regiment, and behind them came a rear-guard, and as that approached Custer shook hands with us and bade us good-by. As he turned to leave us I made some pleasant remark, warning him against being greedy, and with a gay wave of his hand he called back, "No, I will not," and rode off after his command. Little did we think we had seen him for the last time, or imagine under what circumstances we should next see that command, now mounting the bluffs in the distance with its little guidons [light-cavalry pennants] gayly fluttering in the breeze.

[6]This certainly can't be true, as by the time the 7th reached the Little Bighorn, there were horses "giving out."

A very heavy cold wind was blowing from the north, and our steamer did not start until 4 o'clock in the afternoon. We ran on till near dusk, when we tied up for the night and took in wood. The next day (23d) we ran steadily all day, and just before night we tied up, the captain stating that he was unable to reach Fort Pease before dark. We arrived there, however, early the next morning, and my command being in position was at once ferried across the river, and at 5 o'clock started on its march up the Big Horn. I had been attacked with very severe illness the night before, had remained in bed all day and was unable to move. General Terry accompanied the command in person, leaving me on board to meet the column at the mouth of the Little Big Horn. The next day at noon (25th) we entered the mouth of that stream, the *Far West* being the first steamer that ever ploughed its waters, and running till dark tied up for the night, little dreaming what a disastrous day had closed over the gallant Custer and his command. The next morning we were early under way again. The river, which was very full, began to be intersected with numerous islands, and the boat experienced some difficulty in finding a navigable channel. We had just finished pulling over a bar, and were approaching a difficult rapid, when two horsemen were seen on the bluffs coming towards us. They were soon made out to be one of my staff* officers and an orderly. He came aboard and informed me that the infantry part of the command was only a few miles up the river; that they had had a terrible march the day before over the rough mountainous region lying between the Big Horn and Tullock's Fork, during which the men suffered very much from exhaustion and the want of water, and that General Terry, with the cavalry and Gatling guns, had started ahead for a night's march the evening before. This looked as if he anticipated meeting with Indians, and as I now began to be impatient lest the boat would be unable to reach the mouth of the Little Big Horn that day, I determined to mount my horse and overtake the command at once. It was lucky I did so, for the command was not again in communication with the boat until four days afterwards. After a brisk ride of four or five miles I overtook the infantry marching over a plateau not particularly rough, but intersected by numerous deep ravines, which must have rendered the march of the cavalry the night before very tedious and slow, as the night was dark and rainy. Later in the day we overtook the cavalry as it was leaving the place where it had bivouacked at midnight, and on reaching the head of the column and receiving the command from General Terry, I was informed that our scouts reported Indians in front in the direction of the Little Big Horn. Soon after, the officer in charge of the scouts reported that several Indians had been seen to whom the Crows gave chase, and that they had fled across the Big Horn. In their flight they had dropped articles which showed them to be Crows and not Sioux, and our scouts declared them to be some of the Crows which I had lent General Custer at the mouth of the Rosebud for scouting purposes. They were directed to communicate with their friends across the Big Horn, bring them back, and ascertain what news they brought from Custer. For, of course, the inference was at once drawn that these Crows had been sent out by Custer to communicate with our column. We were utterly unprepared for the startling report which our Crows brought back after calling across to their friends on the opposite bank of the Big Horn. Our best interpreter had been left sick at the mouth of the river, and from what we could make out by the indifferent one with us, who appeared very much excited and demoralized by the news, Custer's command had been entirely cut to pieces by the Sioux, who, so said the interpreter, "were chasing our soldiers all over the hills and killing them like buffalo."

This startling piece of news was received with incredulity by every one, and the absconding Crows were again sent for, to come back that we might question them, and try to ascertain something near the facts. Whilst the head of the column was halting for the infantry to close up, General Terry and myself walked over to the edge of the bluff overlooking the valley of the Big Horn to await the return of the scouts, and ascertain from them such news as we could. The broad river intersected by numerous wooded islands was spread out at our feet, and from the edge of a piece of timber nearest us our scouts were soon seen emerging, and approaching a buffalo trail which led up the bluffs to the spot where we were standing. As they came nearer we detected signs of grief; and as old "Show-his-face" (the senator) mounted the steep slope on his pony, he was seen to be crying as if his heart was broken, with great tears streaming down his old weather-beaten face, and uttering every now and then the most doleful exclamations. We had become used to this after seeing them cry at the loss of their horses, and therefore did not attach much importance to it; but when the others arrived and confirmed the previous report, with the information that their friends declared their horses and themselves were too exhausted to cross the river again, and positively refused to come back, it became manifest that the Indians themselves believed in the truth of the report as they heard it.

Of course there was but one thing for us to do, which was to push forward as rapidly as possible and try and clear up for ourselves the terrible uncertainty; for, at all events, the fact seemed undoubted that Custer had come in contact with the Indians, and the sooner we could reach him the better. The march was at once resumed, and we shortly reached the bluffs overlooking the valley of the Little Big Horn, some distance up which huge columns of smoke could now be plainly seen. As we wound along over the rough broken hills seeking for a place to get down into the valley,

I observed that all our Crows, instead of travelling well to the front, as was their custom, stuck close to the column. I ordered the interpreter to take them to the front and report for duty with the advanced guard; but he declared his inability to get them to go, and was evidently himself so badly scared that he produced a bad effect upon the Indians. Finding I could not get them to the front I angrily ordered them to the rear of the column, an order which they obeyed with so much alacrity under the lead of the white interpreter that we saw them no more; and they never stopped till they reached their agency a hundred miles away. This, of course, we ascertained afterwards. They were evidently very badly stampeded, but I attributed this more to the demoralized condition of the white interpreter than to any want of courage on their part; and they afterwards assured me, when they rejoined us at the mouth of the Big Horn, that the interpreter had told them that I said I did not want them any longer.

We had to remain for some time on the high bluffs overlooking the valley of the Little Big Horn, up which the smoke of the fires continued constantly to increase in volume, which gave rise to the hope that, as our guides expressed it, Custer had "got away" with the camp and was destroying it. Such a hope was in consonance with our ideas, for I do not suppose there was a man in the column who entertained for a moment the idea that there were

Indians enough in the country to defeat, much less annihilate, the fine regiment of cavalry which Custer had under his command. Distances in this clear, rarefied atmosphere are very deceptive, and, as we moved on, the distance to the smoke which at first appeared to be only a few miles seemed to lengthen out and grow greater under the weary feet of our men, and when we did finally make our way down into the valley and cross the stream at a deep ford we were still some twelve or fifteen miles from the nearest smoke. To afford rest and food to both men and animals the command was halted here; the animals permitted to graze for an hour and a half and the men to make coffee. In the meantime efforts were made to communicate by courier with General Custer, General Terry offering a large reward to any one who would carry through a dispatch. Two of our guides, Bostwick and Taylor, although unacquainted with the country volunteered for the service, and, shortly after they left, the column resumed its march up the broad open valley. After we had proceeded several miles some stray ponies were picked up by the advance guard, which were evidently estrays from an Indian camp. On our left ran the stream bordered with timber and brushwood, and some distance on our right the valley was bounded by low rolling hills. In our front the stream after cutting into the bluffs crossed the valley from right to left, the timber shutting out all view beyond, save above its top appeared a sharp mountain peak, on the edges of which could now and then be indistinctly made out a few moving figures, and just

51

beyond this peak the smoke appeared to have its origin. Up to this time no Indians had been seen, but shortly after one of our couriers came riding in from the front, and reported that in attempting to reach Custer's command he had run into a number of Indians in the hills,[7] and was unable to proceed farther. A company of cavalry was now thrown out to the hills on our right, and the column pushed forward as rapidly as the men could march, the infantry responding with alacrity and almost keeping up in pace with the horses. Small scattered bands now began to make their appearance on the tops of the distant hills up the river where the latter began to deflect its course to the northward, and as it grew dark more of them could be seen in the distance.

[7]At this time, the vast village at the Little Bighorn battlefield would have been made aware of Terry and Gibbon's approaching columns.

The condition of affairs regarding Custer's command was now more involved in doubt than ever. If he had defeated the Indians and destroyed their camp, as the fires seemed to indicate, it was difficult to account for the presence of these Indians in our front, who were evidently watching us; whereas, if the report of the Crows was correct, and the Indians had defeated Custer, their bearing was equally inexplicable. This state of doubt was only increased when our other courier came in and reported the result of his attempts to get through to Custer. He had struck into the hills to the southward, and had encountered Indians, who appeared to be friendly, and responded to the signals he made them. He approached some of them on foot, and leading his horse, when one of them he said treacherously fired a shot at him, and he fiercely declared he had recognized him as one of Custer's Ree scouts, and that he would kill him when he met him for firing at him. As night closed around us the command was halted and bivouacked in the open prairie; the scouting parties were called in, who reported seeing quite a large number of Indians on the distant hills, but in the gathering darkness nothing could be plainly made out. After watering and grazing the animals they were all carefully picketed inside the command formed in a square, guards established just outside, and the tired men sank to rest eight miles from the brave little band of fellow soldiers which, unknown to us, was watching and waiting on those bleak bluffs of the river above.

Every one was astir at the first appearance of day, and after a hurried breakfast of hardtack, bacon, and coffee, the march was resumed up the valley. The trail, forced into the hills on the right by the encroachment of the river, led through rough ground around a bend in the stream, and as the view opened into the valley beyond, we caught sight, through the scattered timber, of a couple of Indian teepies standing in the open valley. The advance guard with flankers out on the hills to the right now moved rapidly to the front, whilst a party of mounted infantry, which had crossed the river, scouted the hills on that side. As soon as the. Gatling guns were passed over the rough portion of the trail, the whole command, well closed up, moved in compact order up through the open valley beyond, every one eagerly pressing forward and anxious to solve the dread doubt which seemed to hang over the fate of our comrades. Silence reigned around us, only a few distant horsemen had been seen, and, but for the presence of a few scattering Indian ponies, the valley seemed to be entirely deserted. The company of cavalry in the advance was seen to push more rapidly to the front, past the Indian teepies, which showed no life, and on beyond at a gallop, whilst our more slowly moving column seemed merely to crawl along. At length we reached the teepies, found them occupied by dead Indians laid out in state, and surrounded in every direction with the remnants and various odds and ends of a hastily abandoned camp. Teepie poles, skins, robes, pots, kettles, and pans lay scattered about in every direction. But we had little time or inclination to comment on these sights, for every thought was now bent upon the possible fate of our fellow-soldiers, and the desire was intense to solve as soon as possible the dread doubt which now began to fill all minds. For, in searching about amongst the rubbish, some one had picked up a pair of bloody drawers, upon which was plainly written the words, "Sturgis's 7th Cavalry," whilst a buckskin shirt, recognized as belonging to Lieutenant Porter, was discovered with a bullet-hole passing through it.

It was plainly to be seen now that a conflict had indeed taken place, but of its extent or results we were still in as much doubt as ever, when a report came to me from the scouting party in the hills to our left that several dead horses had been discovered in a ravine in that direction. Every eye was now strained to the utmost in search of information, and whilst looking up the valley I caught sight of something on the top of a hill far beyond the sharp peak before referred to, which at once attracted my attention and a closer scrutiny. I sprang from my horse, and with a field glass looked long and anxiously at a number of dark objects which might be either animals or stubby cedar trees. The closest scrutiny failed to detect any movement amongst them, and yet I could not divest my mind of the idea that they were horses, and called upon a pair of younger eyes to try the glass. One of General Terry's staff officers took the glass and seating himself on the ground peered long and anxiously at the spots, but finally said "they are not animals." But scarcely had the words escaped him, when we both noticed a very apparent increase in the number of objects on the highest point of the hill, and now one doubt was solved only to give rise to another. Were the objects seen friends or foes? Had we come in time to save some of our friends, or were the objects on the hill simply a party of Indians watching our approach after having, as the Crows said, destroyed them all? The feeling of anxiety was overwhelming, and the column seemed to crawl along more slowly than ever. The advance was moving ahead fast enough now, and I dispatched a staff officer in haste to ascertain and bring back any information it may have picked up; for I had observed on the peak before spoken of, and opposite which the advanced guard had now arrived, three horsemen evidently observing our movements and watching us closely. They could scarcely, I thought, be white men, for our troops were marching up the valley in two columns, in plain sight of where they sat on their horses, and if friendly they surely would have come down and communicated with us. They did finally come slowly down to a lower hill standing nearer to the river, but there they halted again and seemed to question us with their eyes.

Whilst watching these lookouts and wondering at their strange movements, the officer in charge of the mounted infantry party, in the hills to the north of us, rode up to where General Terry and I sat upon our horses, and his voice trembled as he said, "I have a very sad report to make. I have counted one hundred and ninety-seven dead bodies lying in the hills!" "White men?" was the first question asked. "Yes, white men." A look of horror was upon every face, and for a moment no one spoke. There could be no question now. The Crows were right, and Custer had met with a disaster, but the extent of it was still a matter of doubt; and as we turned our eyes towards the lookouts on the hill above us, as though to question them, we saw them moving, still slowly, however, down closer to the river. Then as they reached a gentle slope they rode on a little faster, and were seen to approach the advance guard, and some one in our anxious group exclaimed, "They are white men!" From out of the timber near the point, a horseman at full speed was now seen coming towards us. It was my staff officer coming with news, and as he approached us on the full run he called out, "I have seen scouts from Colonel Reno, who report their regiment cut to pieces, and Colonel Reno fortified in the bluffs with the remnant." We were still some distance, probably a mile and a half from the objects we had been observing on the hill, and now pushed forward more eagerly than ever, the advance guard being already opposite their position. After we had gone about a mile a party of horsemen was seen approaching, and as we rode forward to meet them we recognized two young officers of the Seventh Cavalry, followed by several orderlies. Hands were grasped almost in silence, but we questioned eagerly with our eyes, and one of the first things they uttered was, "Is General Custer with you?" On being told that we had not seen him, they gave us hurriedly an account of the operations of the past two days, and the facts began to dawn upon us. No one of the party which accompanied General Custer when the command was divided, about noon on the 25th, had been seen by the survivors, and our inference was that they were all, or nearly all, lying up in the hills where our scouting party had found the dead bodies.

Whilst General Terry accompanied the officers to Colonel Reno's position on the hill, I proceeded to select a camp for the command. Nearly the whole valley was black and smoking with the fire which had swept over it, and it was with some difficulty I could find grass sufficient for our animals, as it existed only in spots close to the stream where too green to burn.[8] Except the fire, the ground presented but few evidences of the conflict which had taken place. Now and then a dead horse was seen; but as I approached a bend of the creek (for it is little more than a creek), just below the hill occupied by the troops, I came upon the body of a soldier lying on his face near a dead horse. He was stripped, his scalp gone, his head beaten in, and his body filled with bullet holes and arrows. Close by was another body, also close to a dead horse, lying, like the other, on its face, but partially clothed, and this was recognized by one of our officers as the body of Captain McIntosh. More bodies of both men and horses were found close by, and it was noted that the bodies of men and horses laid almost always *in pairs,* and as this was the ground over which Colonel Reno's command retired towards the hills after its charge down the valley, the inference was drawn, that in the run the horses must have been killed first, and the riders after they fell.

[8]The departing Indians had burned the grasslands and continued setting covering fires in their retreat.

The command was placed in camp here, and details at once set to work to haul away the dead horses and bury the men, both of which were already becoming offensive. Then mounting my horse I proceeded to visit Colonel Reno's command. As I rode a few hundred yards up the river towards the ford, bodies of men and horses were seen scattered along at intervals, and in the river itself several dead horses were lying. The banks of the river at the ford were steep and some six or eight feet high, with here and there an old buffalo trail leading down to the water. The water itself was not over a horse's knee, and close to the bank, on the other side, a series of steep bluffs, intersected at short intervals by steep and narrow ravines, rose up for probably a hundred feet. Up the sides of these ravines, winding about to make the ascent more gradual, numerous paths led, now tramped hard and smooth by the many animals which had recently passed over them. My horse struggled up the steep path, wide enough only for a single animal, with difficulty, and on emerging from the ravine up which it led, I found myself on a sort of rough broken plateau, which sloped gradually up to the curved summit occupied by the troops. I soon came to a line of rifle-pits facing the space I was crossing, and running from the summit of the ridge down to the bluff overlooking the river, whilst behind this and facing the other way was another line, running in a similar way along the summit of an almost parallel ridge. Between the two were standing and lying, almost motionless, the horses and pack-mules of the command. As I approached the summit of the main ridge which overlooked all the rest of the ground I have described, the evidences of the severe struggle which had taken place here began to manifest themselves. Dead horses and mules were lying about in every direction, and in one little depression on the other slope of the main divide I counted forty-eight dead animals. Here and there, these had evidently been made use of as breastworks, and along the top of the ridge holes and rifle-pits extended, connecting the two lines before referred to. On the far side of the ridge, the ground gradually fell away in lower ridges, behind which the Indians had sheltered themselves and their ponies during the fight.

Standing on top of the main ridge with my back to the river, I overlooked the whole of the ground to the front; but on turning to my left, the ground was seen to rise higher and higher in successive ridges which ran nearly perpendicular to the stream, until they culminated in the sharp peak referred to in my description of the previous day upon which we had seen objects at a great distance down the valley. Several of these ridges commanded in reverse the position occupied by the troops, and we were told had been occupied by the Indians during the fight of the 26th, their long-range rifles covering all the space within the lines. Turning again to the left so as to face the river, the broad open flat where Colonel Reno had made his charge at the commencement of the battle on the 25th lay directly at our feet, whilst off towards the south the bluffs which bordered the valley rose up abruptly, and were succeeded by a gently sloping country intersected by several small valleys, with brushwood lining the now dry beds of the streams at the bottoms, while in the far distance the rugged range of the Big Horn Mountains rose, their tops partially covered with snow. One of the little valleys referred to was pointed out to us as the place where at dusk, the evening before, the last of the Indians disappeared in the distance after passing over, in admirable order and in full view of the command, the rolling plateau which bordered the valley of the Little Big Horn to the southward. Looking down the river in the direction we had come was a point of timber jutting out into the plain, where for a portion of the time the cavalry had fought dismounted; and beyond this, in plain sight from where I stood, was located the village where the fight began; and opposite that, hidden from sight by the high peak so often referred to, was the scene of Custer's fight, where his body was found surrounded by those of his men and horses.

On the highest point of the ridge occupied by the troops, and along what had been the northern line of defence, were pitched a number of shelter tents, and under and about these were lying some fifty wounded men, receiving the care of the surgeons and their attendants. The cheerfulness of these poor fellows under their sufferings, and their evident joy at their rescue was touching in the extreme, and we listened with full hearts to their recital in feeble tones of the long anxious hours of waiting and fighting, during which every eye was strained, looking for the coming succor, hoping for its arrival, yet fearing it would be too late. At one time, so strongly did the imagination affect the judgment, the whole command was convinced that columns of troops could be seen moving over the hills to their assistance, but in directly the *opposite* direction from which they actually came. So strong was this delusion that the buglers of the whole command were assembled and ordered to sound their bugles to attract attention. When we finally made our appearance down the valley, the same thing was done, and it is supposed that it was the gathering together of the buglers on the highest point of the hill which finally decided in our minds that we were looking at men and horses, and not clumps of cedar trees. But we heard nothing of the bugles, for the wind was blowing from us.

Standing on the scene of the conflict, we heard from officers and men the story of the struggle and their experience for the past forty-eight hours. The battle commenced some time about noon on the 25th by the charge of the three companies down towards the village. They reached the point of timber I have referred to as jutting out into the plain. Here they were dismounted for a time and fought from the timber, and then when the Indians came swarming around them from the ravines in the bluffs, they mounted again, and then commenced the race for the bluffs bordering the river. It must, from their description, have been a race of life against death. Look up the stream, and you will see the ford where Reno's command crossed to enter the fight. The one it crossed to reach its present position lies directly at your feet. Turning now to the left again so as once more to place your back to the river, and looking up to your right and front, you can trace with the eye a little valley winding its way up into the broken ground to the northeast. It was down this valley that Custer's command approached the Little Big Horn, and near where it joins the valley of that stream is the ford where Reno crossed before the battle. Before reaching that point, Custer, it appears by his trail, turned to the right with his five companies, skirted along through these hills to our front, passed to the right of the sharp peak, and still on, beyond it and out of sight of where we stand. His trail is all that is left to tell the story of his route, for no white man of all those who accompanied him has since been seen alive. To us who stand upon the ground and make these observations, his fate is still a matter of doubt, and is now to be solved. One of Colonel Reno's companies is mounted and started for the scene of Custer's fight. It leaves our position, and winding along the rolling hills, ascends the high ground to the right of the high peak, and disappears beyond, just as Custer's command would have vanished probably from the sight of an observer standing where we are now.

Whilst this company is away we are busy preparing to remove the wounded down from the hot, dusty hill where they are lying to my camp, where they will be more comfortable and can be better cared for.

After being absent a couple of hours the detached company is seen winding its way back, and as it approaches we all collect round General Terry to hear the report of its gray-haired captain, who won such praises by his indomitable bearing in the fight [Captain Frederick Benteen]. He comes forward, dismounts, and in a low, very quiet voice, tells his story. He had followed Custer's trail to the scene of the battle opposite the main body of the Indian camp, and amid the rolling hills which borders the river-bank on the north. As he approached the ground scattered bodies of men and horses were found, growing more numerous as he advanced. In the midst of the field a long *backbone* ran out obliquely back from the river, rising very gradually until it terminated in a little knoll which commanded a view of all the surrounding ground, and of the Indian camp-ground beyond the river. On each side of this backbone, and sometimes on top of it, dead men and horses were scattered along. These became more numerous as the terminating knoll was reached; and on the southwestern slope of that lay the brave Custer surrounded by the bodies of several of his officers and forty or fifty of his men, whilst horses were scattered about in every direction. All were stripped, and most of the bodies were scalped and mutilated. And now commenced the duty of recognizing the dead. Of Custer there could be no doubt. He was lying in a perfectly natural position as many had seen him lying when asleep, and, we were told, was not at all mutilated, and that, only after a good deal of search the wounds of which he died could be found. The field was searched and one after another the officers were found and recognized, all except two. A count of the bodies disclosed the fact that some twenty-five or thirty were missing, and we could not, until some time afterwards, form even a surmise in regard to their fate.[9]

[9]As of 2014, they have not been found, although archaeologists who have worked at the site believe they may be in Deep Ravine, southwest of Last Stand Hill.

The great mystery was now solved, at last, of the destruction of that part of Custer's command. It was possible that some few individuals might have escaped the general massacre; but so far as we could judge all had fallen; and the particulars of that sad and desperate conflict against overwhelming numbers of the savage horde which flocked about Custer and his devoted three hundred when Reno was beaten back, will probably never be known.

THE END.

HUNTING SITTING BULL.

THE poor wounded claimed my first care. They were lying on the hot dusty hill under inadequate shelter, and steps were at once taken to remove them to my cooler, pleasanter camp on the creek-bank below. The majority of them had to be carried, and there was not a single stretcher or litter in the command. These had therefore to be improvised. A quantity of the light teepie poles were collected from the Indian camp, and by means of these, old pieces of canvas, and blankets, a number were made, and by night all the wounded were carried down the steep slope of the bluffs, across the creek, and down to our camp, the men working by relays.

The Seventh Cavalry remained upon the bluffs during the night, and early the next morning moved down to the scene of Custer's conflict, to perform the mournful duty of burying the remains of their slaughtered comrades. This would have been an impracticable task but for the discovery, in the deserted Indian camp, of a large number of shovels and spades, by the aid of which the work was performed.

The formidable question of the transportation of the wounded now came up and had to be met. The mouth of the Little Big Horn to which point the steamer *Far West* had been ordered, was some twenty miles distant, and couriers had been dispatched to communicate with her, ascertain if she had reached there, and warn her to await our arrival. In the meantime, we set to work to construct the necessary litters with what rough material could be collected. Lieutenant D., of the Second Cavalry, volunteered to construct *horse-litters* out of rough cottonwood poles, rawhide, and ropes, but the process proved a very slow and tedious one, and other details were set to work collecting teepie poles and manufacturing hand-litters out of them and such old canvas as was to be had. Late in the afternoon, but four or five of the horse-litters had been finished, and the necessary number was completed with hand- litters. But on trying the mules in the horse-litters (all of them animals taken from baggage-wagons, unused to carrying packs, and sore from their few days' service under the saddles), most of them proved so refractory in the novel position assigned them, that grave doubts arose as to whether the suffering wounded could be safely carried in this way.

It was to be feared that any show of precipitancy in leaving our position was calculated to invite an attack from the overwhelming number of our enemies, and we should probably not have started that day at all, but for the report of the surgeons that it was indispensable that the wounded should be removed at once to avoid the ill effects of the heat, and the flies that swarmed around them in immense numbers from the dead bodies in the vicinity. It was therefore decided late in the afternoon to commence the movement, and as the sun sank behind the western hills, the wounded were transferred to the litters and the sad cortege moved out of camp.

At first two men were assigned to each hand-litter, but it was soon found that this was not sufficient, and the number had to be doubled, and, besides, two men had to be assigned to each horse- litter to steady it. Infantrymen and dismounted cavalrymen relieved each other every few minutes, but our progress was slow and laborious, and before we had made more than a mile from our camp, darkness overtook our straggling and disorganized column, completely broken up by the repeated halts and constantly recurring changes of carriers.

As we moved through the darkness, the silence of night broken only by the tramp of men and horses and the groans of the suffering wounded, I could not help contrasting the scene presented with that gay spectacle we had witnessed only six days before, when Custer's splendid regiment moved out in solid column, with its guidons fluttering in the breeze as it disappeared from our sight over the bluffs at the mouth of the Rosebud.

Long, tedious, and slow, the hours of that sad night wore on, and it was past midnight before we reached camp at a distance of only four and a half miles.

A company of the Second Cavalry had been sent out in the morning to make a reconnoissance on the trail of the retreating Indians. It was followed some ten or twelve miles, leading directly south towards the Big Horn

Mountains, and was there found to divide, one portion going to the southeast, the other to the southwest, and the whole country in those directions was filled with the smoke of fires, lit either as signals or to burn the grass in rear of the retreating camps. In returning to our camp, the scouting party struck across to the Little Big Horn, coming down which was discovered a large lodge-pole trail, only a day or two old. From this it was inferred that General Custer had fought not only the party whose trail he had followed over from the Rosebud, but also the warriors of another large camp which before the fight had formed a junction with it, by coming up from the south, in which direction, as we afterward learned, General Crook had had his fight on the 17th, only eight days previous to Custer's battle. The concentration of superior numbers, thus effected, demonstrated very clearly that the Sioux leader, whoever he was, was not lacking in those strategic ideas justly deemed so valuable in civilized warfare. From these indications it would appear that, after the check given General Crook on the 17th, the whole hostile force concentrated against Custer, who by an almost unheard-of rapidity of movement had precipitated himself against their main camp. We know absolutely nothing of the details of the conflict, as relates to that portion of the command under Custer's personal supervision, but so soon as his part was annihilated, the whole hostile force turned upon the balance of the command, and laid siege to that upon the bluffs, where it was closely confined until the afternoon of the next day, when, upon the approach of our column, the whole Indian force decamped.

From the top of the peak, overlooking Colonel Reno's position, an observer could see far down the valley of the Little Big Horn, and the Indians probably had early news of our approach, and no doubt knew of our coming when we were fifteen or twenty miles away.

They were doubtless much elated by the total annihilation of Custer's part of the force, and made repeated and persistent efforts to complete their victory by destroying the rest of the command. But these were manfully and desperately resisted, and the Indians, incumbered with their camp equipage and families, doubtless felt no desire to continue the struggle with fresh troops, although these numerically were only about as strong as the force they were then fighting. Our arrival, therefore, was opportune; although, had it been possible to anticipate it by thirty-six or even twenty-four hours, the result doubtless would have been even more satisfactory. As it was, we were joyfully hailed as deliverers, and many did not hesitate to express the opinion that but for our arrival they would all have shared a common fate. This was especially noticeable in the wounded, who appeared to feel that they were stepping from death back to life again. Poor fellows! an impression had, in some way, gained a footing amongst them during the long weary hours of the fight on the 26th that, to save the balance of the command, they were to be abandoned. Hence, *their* joy at our arrival can better be imagined than described. I have seen in the course of my military life many wounded men, but I never saw any who endured suffering, privations, and the fatigue of travel, more patiently and cheerfully than those brave fellows of the Seventh Cavalry.

Our march of four and a half miles on the 28th demonstrated that it was practically out of the question, to transport the wounded in anything like a reasonable time in the hand-litters, and, as the command laid over the next day for the purpose of destroying the large quantity of property left behind in the Indian camp, the delay was taken advantage of to construct, under the superintendence of Lieutenant D., an additional number of mule-litters, the few he had made the day before having worked satisfactorily. Ash poles were obtained, several dead horses lying about the camp were skinned for rawhide, and by the afternoon nearly the requisite number was completed, the full number being made up by structures called "travoii's," or "travailles," in imitation of the Indian method. These consist of a couple of lodge poles, having one end fastened to the saddle of a packhorse, and the other trailing on the ground, the two being fastened together just behind the tail of the horse by a wicker-work platform, on which the patient reclines. The light flexible poles act as springs, and, except over very rough ground, the movement is far from disagreeable or rough. All the animals of the pack-train were now picked

71

over, and the most gentle and best broken of these were turned over to Lieutenant D. for service with the litters.

A number of companies were now sent out, scattered all over the site of the camp, to collect and destroy the property left by the Indians, and soon columns of smoke were seen rising in every direction from burning lodge-poles, upon which were thrown vast quantities of robes, dressed skins of different kinds, and other inflammable objects, while such pans, kettles, cups, and *crockery,* as were not needed by the troops were broken up.

Up to this time 1 had no opportunity to personally visit the scene of Custer's battle, and taking advantage of our delay in camp, which was situated just below and beyond the limits of the old Indian camp, I that morning rode up to the spot, and went over most of the ground.

The Little Big Horn is a stream with some singular features. It winds through its valley in a very crooked bed, bordered in many places with high precipitous banks, and is generally through this part of its course very sluggish, and wherever this is the case the water is deep enough to swim a horse. At various intervals between these sluggish parts the water becomes shallow enough to admit of fording, and goes rippling along to form the next deep spot below. About a mile below the bluffs occupied by Colonel Reno's command the river makes a considerable bend to the northward, and, sweeping round towards the south again, cuts in its course well into the bluff on the north bank, and leaves all the valley on the south bank. In this curve the Indian camp was located, and on the river just below its site, and at the most southern point on the curve, our present camp is situated. Close by us are two such fords as I have described, and crossing one of these we move up the right bank of the stream which here runs nearly due south. On our right is the wooded bank of the river, the intervening space between the cottonwood trees being filled up with brushwood. On our left the valley opens out into a grass-covered prairie, fringed on its southern side, and again on its western side, where the stream curves to the north again, with timber and brushwood. Riding along up the stream we come to the point where, after cutting the bluffs skirting it on the north, it turns sharply to the south. Here the ground commences to rise before us in gently sloping hills separated by little valleys, one of which seems to lead in about the direction we want to take. Just before this valley joins the valley of the river, the bottom has been cut into a gulch some eight or ten feet deep, and this is filled with brushwood nourished by the moisture of the rain-water, which doubtless cut out the gulch. Struck with the fact that this little valley seemed to be a natural outlet from the scene of the fight, and the possibility that individuals might have sought shelter in the gulch on their way to the timber below, we closely examined the place up to the point where the gulch headed, but found no "signs." As we proceeded up the valley, now an open grassy slope, we suddenly came upon a body lying in the grass. It was lying upon its back, and was in an advanced state of decomposition. It was not stripped, but had evidently been scalped and one ear cut off. The clothing was not that of a soldier, and, with the idea of identifying the remains, I caused one of the boots to be cut off and the stocking and drawers examined for a name, but none could be found. On looking at the boot, however, a curious construction was observed. The heel of the boot was reinforced by a piece of leather which in front terminated in two straps, one of which was furnished with a buckle, evidently for the purpose of tightening the instep of the boot. This led to the identification of the remains, for on being carried to camp the boot was recognized as one belonging to Mr. Kellogg, a newspaper correspondent who accompanied General Custer's column. Beyond this point the ground commenced to rise more rapidly, and the valley was broken up into several smaller ones which lead up towards the higher ground beyond. Following up one of these we reach a rolling but not very broken space, the ground rising higher and higher until it reaches a culminating knoll dominating all the ground in the immediate vicinity. This knoll, by common consent now called Custer's Hill, is the spot where his body was found surrounded by those of several of his officers and some forty or fifty of his men. We can see from where we are numerous bodies of dead horses scattered along its southwestern slope, and as we ride up towards it, we come across another body lying in a depression just as if killed whilst using his rifle there. We follow the sloping ground bearing a little to the left or westward until we reach the top, and then look around us. On the very top are four or five dead horses, swollen, putrid, and offensive, their stiffened limbs sticking straight out from their bodies. On the slope beyond others are thickly lying in all conceivable positions, and dotted about on the ground in all directions are little mounds of freshly turned earth, showing where each brave soldier sleeps his last sleep. Close under the brow of the knoll several horses are lying nearer together than the rest, and by the side of one of these we are told the body of Custer was found. The top of the knoll is only a few feet higher than the general surface of the long straight ridge, which runs off obliquely towards the river, in the direction of that ford at which it is supposed Custer made the attempt to cross.

Before leaving the prominent point from which probably Custer surveyed his last battle and took his farewell of earth, let us look around us. There is no point within rifle range which we do not overlook, but the surrounding space, which only a few days ago resounded with the sharp rattle of rifles and the wild yells of savages, is now silent as the grave, and filled with the fetid odor of decaying bodies.

Looking first along the ridge, which, almost level, runs off as straight as an arrow, the eye catches sight on both slopes of dead horses lying here and there, and little mounds showing where the riders fell and are lying. Beyond the end of this, in the direction of the ford, the ground becomes more broken, but still only in gentle slopes as it descends towards the river. Far beyond, a little to the left, rises that peak so often referred to, which with its neighboring heights hides from our sight the bluffs where Reno was besieged. Turning now to the right and facing the river, the ground is seen to be broken up into rolling hills and valleys, the sides formed of gentle slopes, but now and then where these valleys approach the river their bottoms are washed into gulches sometimes ten or fifteen feet deep. One is especially noted, to the right and front, running in a direction nearly perpendicular to the river, and at the bottom of this one were found some forty or fifty bodies. The general surface of the ground does not slope off towards the river, but continues high up to the very bank and above it; here and there the eye catches sight of the tops of the trees bordering the stream, and, beyond, the site of the Indian village. Turning now our backs upon the river, we see the ground sloping off rapidly behind the position into a long open valley, the lower part of which, as it runs off to join the valley of the Little Big Horn, far below, is seen to be fringed with brushwood, and an examination of this discloses the presence of innumerable pony tracks. More to the right, and beyond the little valley which borders on the north the straight ridge referred to, the ground rises into another ridge, and beyond this, as far as the eye can reach, extends a mass of rough broken "bad lands." Had we only known what dread secret those bad lands were hiding, we probably should have been able to perform the mournful duty of interring the remains of our twenty-five or thirty missing comrades. But we knew nothing of this then, and, turning our horses' heads, rode slowly along the top of the main ridge, stopping now and then to examine the place where some poor wounded animal, struggling in its death throes, had worked its way down the slope to the valley below. Arrived at the end of the ridge the ground opens out where several other ridges join it into a kind of level platform. Here evidently a severe struggle took place, for the bodies of men and horses are thickly strewn about. Moving to the far edge of this irregular plateau the ground is seen to fall away in a gently sloping valley towards the ford over which Custer is supposed to have attempted a crossing. I have stated that the top of Custer's Hill dominates over the whole surrounding country. Standing upon that he must have had a full view of the struggle taking place around him, and of the Indian village lying at his feet, but not within his power. And when forced back by overwhelming numbers, only to find the valley behind filled also with yelling hordes of savages, he must, whilst straining his eyes in that direction from which alone help could come, have recognized when too late the courageous-born error he committed in dividing his force in the presence of so numerous an enemy.

The body of our poor guide, Mitch Bouyer, was found lying in the midst of the troopers, slain, as the Sioux had several times reported they had slain him, in battle. He was a half-breed Sioux, and they had often tried to kill him. He was the protégé and pupil of the celebrated guide Jim Bridger; was the best guide in this section of the country, and the only half-breed I ever met who could give the distances to be passed over with any accuracy *in miles.*

The bodies of all the officers but two were found and recognized, and those of all the men, except some twenty or thirty, accounted for. The probable fate of these will be hereafter referred to. By the burial-place of each officer was driven to the head a stake, in the top of which a hole was bored, and in this was placed a paper having upon it the name and rank of the officer.

On leaving the battle-ground we bore obliquely to the right, and making our way over the steep bluffs down to the river, near the mouth of the deep gulch mentioned as containing so many of our dead troopers, pushed our way through the brushwood of the river- bank, and, crossing the river at a shallow ford, entered the site of the Indian camp, where our working parties were still busy searching for, collecting, and destroying the Indian property, part of which was found concealed in the brush.

Riding across the valley towards the bluffs, we passed the site of the two teepies filled with dead Indians, now a mass of charred remains, and approached a clump of small trees, in and near which the Indians had buried a number of their dead, the ponies slaughtered in their honor lying about the remains of their dead masters, now tumbled upon the ground from the destruction of the scaffolding by those human ghouls whose existence seems to be inseparable from a fighting force, *after* the fighting is over, and whose vandal acts painfully impress one with the conviction that in war barbarism stands upon a level only a little lower than our boasted modern civilization.

The bodies lay upon the ground, the hideous display of their mortal corruption contrasting strangely with the gay robes and tinsel trappings with which they had been carefully, perhaps lovingly, decked. Turning from this revolting spectacle, we rode back to camp to find the work of litter-making going on bravely and successfully. About the camp numerous mules in couples, between the rude shafts of the litters, were being led about to get accustomed to the awkward movement, and under the direction of the indefatigable Lieutenant D., the men as well as the mules were being instructed how to turn, how to advance? hold back, etc., so that the poor suffering burdens should neither be thrown out nor shaken more roughly than was necessary.

At length all was ready; the wounded were lifted as tenderly as possible into the litters, and at six o'clock in the afternoon we started, expecting to make a short march, more to test the litters than anything else. But we had not gone more than a few miles and had just crossed the river at second time when two horsemen made their appearance on the bluffs on our left, and our couriers rode into the column bringing us news that the "Far West" was waiting for us at the mouth of the Little Big Horn. Our failure to obtain news of these couriers, started from our camp on the morning of the 29th, had caused serious apprehension that they might have fallen into the hands of the hostiles; for the distance they had to travel was only twenty miles, and if unmolested they should have been back to us before. Their return with the good news they bore solved the mystery of the delay. Leaving us late in the afternoon, they rode all night, and just at daylight mounted a hill overlooking the mouth of the Little Big Horn to look for the steamer. She was nowhere to be seen. Then, in accordance with their instructions, they started down the Big Horn to find her, following the bank of the river up and down over the deep gulches which all along the right bank lead into that stream. But their anxious search was without avail, and finally, late in the afternoon, they reached the mouth of the river, communicated with our supply camp there, obtained some food and forage for their horses, and the next morning started back up the Big Horn, and early in the afternoon when they rose the hill at the mouth of the Little Big Horn, a glad sight met their eyes, for there lay the steamer moored to the bank. They were quickly on board, and there learned that the officer in charge of the boat, uncertain as to whether or not he had reached the mouth of the Little Big Horn, directed the captain to run further up the river, which he did for about ten miles, and during the absence of the boat our couriers reached the point where they expected to find her. Resting on board the boat for an hour, the two indefatigable riders mounted their horses again, and finally reached us after a ride of about one hundred and forty miles in the course of forty-eight hours. Their names deserve to be preserved in the records of the campaign. One of them was an orderly of mine, Private Goodwin, of the Seventh Infantry, the other, Bostwick, the post-guide of Fort Shaw. They had a wonderful story to tell us of a Crow Indian, named "Curly," whom they found on the boat, who asserted his escape from the Custer massacre, who had given many particulars of the fight, and even drew a rough map of the ground. The story of this man was found on examination to be consistent and intelligible, and the faithful fellow had ridden from the battle-field, immediately on his escape, to the mouth of the Big Horn, and not finding General Terry there, had followed up the stream to the boat, where he carried the first news of Custer's disaster. There is nothing very remarkable in the fact that a friendly *Indian* should have succeeded in making his escape from the general massacre in the midst of the turmoil of battle, however difficult it might have been for a single *white* man to do so, and Curly removed any lingering hope that any of the troops escaped, by stating that when he left, a party of twenty-five or thirty of our men had succeeded in getting away into the hills, several miles distant, but that they were entirely surrounded by a numerous band of Indians; that he could hear the firing there when he left, and that they were undoubtedly all killed. He described how he threw his blanket over his head, pretended to be a Sioux, and even fired his pistol towards the body of a dead soldier, as the Sioux were doing, and then slipped away from the fight.

Assured now of the close proximity of the boat, and anxious to get the wounded as soon as possible within its comfortable shelter. General Terry decided to push forward at once for the mouth of the stream. The mule-litters were working beyond our most sanguine expectations, both as regarded comfort and rapidity of movement, and all felt that Lieutenant D., by his energy and skill, had relieved us from a difficult dilemma, and our wounded from prolonged suffering. We therefore pushed rapidly down the valley, keeping near the bluffs, for Bostwick informed us that we must mount these and cross a high, wide plateau, before we could reach the boat. Darkness overtook us before we were able to reach this part of our road, but we had a young moon to light us on our way, and pushed ahead, hoping to reach the boat by eleven o'clock or midnight. But on reaching the plateau, the sky was overcast with heavy clouds. It became dark as pitch, and rain commenced to fall. We had now nothing to depend on but our sense of direction, and the skill of our guide, who had come over the ground in the daylight. Now and then the moon broke through the clouds to assure us of our direction, but the slowly moving column was liable to separate at the slightest change of direction in front, and finally, pushing ahead with too much eagerness to find the path down from the plateau to the river, the advance found itself separated from the rest of the column, and we had no recourse but the sound of our bugles to get the command together again. This was finally effected, but amid the darkness and rain, our guide failed to discover the ravine down which our path lay, or to be sure even of his direction, and whilst we were pondering over the difficulty, there came moving to the front one of our Crow scouts, "Half-Yellow-Face," leading behind him a pony with a "travoir" on which was travelling a wounded Crow. Instinctively, for he could understand no English, and we had no interpreter, he seemed to divine what was wanted, took the lead, and we followed him with childlike faith in his skill. But even the Indian's skill was baffled, and he sought in vain in the midst of the rain and darkness to find the pathway down to the river bottom. We followed him closely, for otherwise the column would have been lost amid the windings in and out of the heads of the ravines, and we once found ourselves upon a point bounded on each side by gulches of unknown depth and steepness, and were obliged to countermarch the whole column, at the imminent risk of upsetting the litters, or having them run into each other. In the confusion, indeed, one of the men, a poor fellow whose leg was amputated, had a narrow escape, for one of the mules of his litter stepped into a hole and fell, and brought him with violence to the ground. Our search finally brought us in sight of a light, which would have aided us much, provided we could have gone directly to it, but this we were debarred from doing by the ravines and broken ground, and as the moon went down and the darkness increased, it began to look as if we were not going to reach the boat that night, after all; but the prospect of halting within sight of our harbor of rest, bivouacking on that bleak hill, with such scant accommodations for the wounded, prompted to renewed efforts.

The column was now baited, and in company with a staff officer I rode forward to try and pick out a way. I was soon compelled to dismount" but we finally succeeded in making our way down to a lower level, and whilst going towards the light were hailed by a challenge. In answer to our call, "Who are you?" came back the welcome words, "Captain B., of the Sixth Infantry" (the officer in charge of the boat), and in a few minutes he was mounted on my horse and on his way back to the head of the column, whilst I reached the boat and started men out to build fires along the route. They were all up and expecting us, on the boat; and the lower deck, inclosed with canvas, was prepared with beds to make our wounded as comfortable as possible. It was now long after midnight, the side of the hill was soon ablaze with a line of fires, and by the light of these the litters made their way down, and when dawn commenced to streak the eastern sky, our poor patient sufferers were comfortably at rest on the deck of the *Far West*.

The next day she started down the river, and on the second day thereafter I reached the Yellowstone with the command, and, being ferried across the river, went into camp around our supply train. Here we remained until the 26th of July, receiving in the meantime supplies from down the river by steamer, and mails from Fort Ellis by small boat and carriers. Communication with the main

Crow camp near Pompey's Pillar was opened, and on the 7th a party from there brought us the first news we received of General Crook's fight on the Rosebud on the 17th of June. It was carried to the camp by the Crows who were with General Crook's force in the battle, and two days afterwards we received further news about the fight, in a mail brought by scouts from the mouth of Powder River.

General Terry had been very anxious for some time to communicate with General Crook, and a message was dispatched to the Crows to try and induce them to go through, but none could be found willing to take the risk, although a large reward was offered. Their horses were tired, and they wanted to be with their families, they said. The real reason was, they regarded the trip as too hazardous, from the large number of Sioux known to be in that part of the country. Hearing of what was wanted, one of our citizen teamsters came forward and volunteered to carry a dispatch through. He possessed one thing in an eminent degree—a full knowledge of the law of trade so for as regards supply and demand. For knowing the demand was great, and the supply of couriers small, he thought he had a "comer" on couriers, and placed a very high estimate on his services, demanding in the first place fifteen hundred dollars. Being informed that this would not be paid, he dropped to six hundred, and the use of a horse, a rifle, and a field- glass. On the evening of the 4th of July he was put across the river, and four days afterwards he was back to us without horse, rifle, glass, hat, or shoes, and with a wonderful story of his narrow escape from Indians, and his vain attempt to cross the Little Big Horn on a raft, in which attempt he had lost everything. As his account was not very clear, and the Little Big Horn was known to be an insignificant stream in which it would be difficult to find water enough to float a raft, his story was looked upon with suspicion, and it was even strongly insinuated that he had never left the timber on the south side of the Yellowstone. Volunteers from my command were now called for to go through to General Crook, and in answer twelve men came forward and offered their services. Amongst them were the two men already mentioned as carrying the dispatches to General Terry by boat down the river on the 27th of May, Evans and Stewart, and with them came a third belonging to the same company, Bell, Company "E," Seventh Infantry. I called all these twelve men up, told them what was required, what risks would probably have to be run, and questioned eachjn regard to how he proposed to make the trip. I knew nothing of the qualifications of any of them, so far as their knowledge of woodcraft was concerned, a knowledge so essential to a successful trip through an entirely unknown region. But the answers and bearing of the three men, all from one company, and proposing to go together, finally decided the matter in their favor, and they were told to get ready at once. Evans and Stewart were both tall, gaunt, lank specimens of humanity, and looked as if a hard day's ride would use them up completely. Bell was short, and more stoutly made. All of them appeared to be very quiet men, did not light up at all in conversation, and exhibited no enthusiasm whatever. Evans was apparently the leader of the party, and to him I gave full instructions as to how he was to travel. I also placed in his hand a section of a map of the country he was to pass over, marking upon it the supposed location of General Crook's camp. He looked at this in a stolid sort of way, and I began to think he did not even know the object in giving it to him. But he quietly stowed it away in his pocket, and after he came back to us, told me with a little smile he believed he could go anywhere in an unknown country if he had a map to travel by. They all three provided themselves with moccasins, so as when on foot, to make Indian instead of white man's "sign," and being provided each with a good horse, rifle, plenty of ammunition, and three days' rations, • they were put across the river on the afternoon of Sunday the 9th, being accompanied some miles up the valley of Tullock's Fork by a company of cavalry, which, as night came on, left them to pursue their perilous route, and for sixteen days we heard not a word of news in regard to them.

On General Terry's invitation, some fifty or sixty Crows came down and joined us, and with them came back all the scouts who had left us the morning we heard of the Custer disaster. They all appeared much mortified at their conduct, especially as the Crows who had remained with us had been given a number of Sioux ponies picked up on the trip, which they had exhibited to their companions as trophies of the expedition. I was satisfied on talking with them that their defection was entirely due to the white interpreter who was with them, and who did not return until some time afterwards. Soon after their arrival four of them were induced, after considerable persuasion, to start for General Crook's camp with a duplicate of the dispatch sent by the three soldiers, and on the 17th, having in the meantime "prepared their *medicine,*" they set out, and we heard no more of them for eight days.

The weather during the summer's operations became a matter of comment with all. Accustomed as we were to the exceedingly dry climate of Montana, where, during the summer months, anything more than a slight sprinkling of rain is almost unheard of, and the sound of loud thunder almost unknown, we were unprepared for the perfect deluges of rain which repeatedly overwhelmed us, and . seldom selected our camps with any reference to water, regarding each rainfall as a phenomenon not likely to be repeated. Our present camp was located in the flat open bottom between the river and the bluffs, through which last, just above camp, a large dry gulch ran, having at its mouth a quantity of large driftwood. Where this gulch opened out into the valley the waters in times past, instead of cutting a channel out of the soil, as is usual, seem to have been in the habit of spreading themselves over the whole face of the valley. On the afternoon of the 13th we were visited by a severe storm of rain, accompanied by heavy thunder and lightning, and the next night a terrific rain commenced falling, and during nearly the entire night the whole atmosphere was lit up by vivid flashes of lightning, and resounded with constant peals of thunder. As daylight approached, a stir was heard in camp, and it soon appeared that all the campground, except a few elevated points, was under water, and the men busy removing their bedding and provisions to the higher ground. Wherever ditches were of any avail, men were set to work to dig them, but most of the ground was entirely submerged with some six to eighteen inches of water, and this, far from decreasing when the rain ceased, grew rapidly in depth as the water accumulated from the drainage of the surrounding gravelly hills poured in upon us from the gulch, which was now a raging torrent. It is not pleasant to be flooded out of your blankets at any time by a stream of muddy water from the "bad lands," and we soon changed camp to a more favorable location below Fort Pease.

A mournful incident occurred on the morning of the 19th. One of our officers who had for years suffered with a painful disease, the seeds of which were laid in Libby Prison during the war, rendered, it is supposed, desperate by his sufferings, put an end to his existence by shooting himself through the heart with a pistol. We laid him to rest in the afternoon on the top of a hill overlooking our camp, and piled up stones over his grave to prevent the depredations of wild animals.

Although no Indians had been seen since leaving Custer's battleground, we had reason to suspect we were watched, and on the night of the 19th two were fired upon whilst approaching our pickets, evidently with the design of spying out our camp, and attempting to steal our stock. The country was kept well scouted, too, and evidences were discovered that a party of twenty-five or thirty was prowling about in the vicinity. Having Indians from two different tribes, the Crows and Rees, in our camp, great care was necessary to avoid collision between these and the resultant alarms in camp. One evening whilst quietly resting in camp, some one called attention to a number of horsemen on a distant hill, apparently watching our camp. The Crows, on having their attention attracted to them, immediately became very much excited. They at once stripped for the fight, leaped upon their ponies without saddles, and with rifles in hand started on a helter-skelter run for the bluffs, yelling as they went. We watched them as they crossed the valley on their fleet little ponies, and in an almost incredibly short space of time they were seen rapidly climbing the hills a mile or two away. They disappeared over the top, a shot or two was heard, then all was still, and shortly afterwards the whole party was seen slowly coming back, accompanied by several Rees who had been imprudently permitted to leave camp on a scout, contrary to orders. They had been fired upon by the excited Crows, and found some difficulty in convincing them they were not *hostile* Sioux.

So great a length of time had now elapsed since the departure of Evans, Stewart, and Bell, that all began to look upon it as a matter of course that they had failed in their mission, and to mourn the brave fellows as so many more victims to the barbarous contest. When, therefore, on the 25th horsemen were reported as appearing on the bluffs south of the river, every one was on the alert as to who they were; for they might be either hostiles, taking a view of our camp, or couriers from General Terry, who had gone down to Powder River some days before. Scarcely any one entertained a hope that they were our absent couriers. They soon showed us they were not hostile, and coming down to the bank of the river a boat was sent over to meet them. Then a hope was expressed that they might be our absent men, and as the boat neared the opposite shore the conduct of the crew was narrowly watched through our glasses, for although some of the strangers were seen to be Indians at least two were recognized as white men. When the boat finally reached the shore, and the men in it were seen to cordially grasp the hands of the two white men, we felt sure they were our long- absent couriers and brought us news from General Crook, and when they landed on our shore and presented me with dispatches from General Crook I greeted them almost like men risen from the dead. Bell's horse had broken down on the trip, and Evans and Stewart only returned, accompanied by the Crow scouts, who had also succeeded in getting through to General Crook's camp. The modest recital of these men of their trip through a region swarming with hostiles, was interesting in the extreme. Their conduct was, enthusiastically, commented upon by the whole press of the country, and the Department commander published a highly complimentary order, thanking them for their services. The news they brought decided the plan of our future operations, and two days after their return we commenced the march to the mouth of the Rosebud, where for the present was to be our depot of supplies. The hostile Indians were evidently still in the vicinity of General Crook, near the base of the Big Horn Mountains. We could no longer use the Big Horn River as a line of supply, for the waters were falling, and soon that stream, as well as the Yellowstone, adjacent, would be impracticable for steamboats. Hence the necessity of a depot and starting-point lower down the latter river. Besides which, the valley of the Rosebud could be made practicable for wagons, and led in the direction of the location of the hostiles and of General Crook's position. Starting on the 27th the command joined General Terry it the Rosebud on the 30th, he in the meantime having proceeded there by steamer, to locate the supply camp and the reinforcements known to be coming up the river.

Our new camp was in a flat sandy bottom interspersed with groves of trees. Directly opposite was the mouth of the Rosebud, below which, on a rocky point, were the remains of an old trading post, and on a hill just above it the remains of an old Indian grave, the scaffold of which was tumbling to pieces.

Indians always keep with the greatest care every scrap of writing they can get hold of, believing, I presume, that as white men scrutinize closely all such documents they must be *"good medicine,"* and such things are frequently deposited in the grave-clothes of the dead. A number of articles were picked up about this grave, and as it is possible some of them may serve to clear up the fate of some poor frontiersman, whose family never heard of him after his disappearance in the far West, I will describe what they were. First was a copy of "The Soldier's Hymn-book," such as were distributed among our men during the war. With this was an envelope, addressed

"MRS. M. BETTS,

"Toledo,

"Jama Co.,

"Iowa."

On this there was no postmark, and it evidently had never been mailed; and a second envelope, much soiled and torn, with a stamp, a portion of the Toledo postmark, and this portion of an address:

"BETTS,

"Co. F. Sixth Iowa Cav.,

"Sioux City,

"—ase forward."

A letter, which was probably inclosed in this envelope, was dated "No. 3, June 20th, '64." It commences "Dear

93

husband," is signed "wife," speaks of "Jimmy" having gone to the army, and calls her husband "Duke." Besides this there was a scrap of letter-paper, upon which was written in pencil, "he has 2 pieces of gold, he says it is worth 20 drs. I cannot talk with them so am at a great loss on that account this man has been kind to me but am compelled to do their bidding

"FANNIE KELLY,

"Captive white woman."

A round piece of something which resembles iron pyrites was picked up, and is probably one of the pieces of "gold" referred to.

On the 1st of August six companies of the Twenty-second Infantry arrived by boat, having had a skirmish on the way up at the mouth of Powder River with a party of Indians, and the next day six companies of the Fifth Infantry arrived, and went into camp. All the reinforcements expected immediately having now arrived, the movement across the Yellowstone commenced on the 3d, and was completed on the 7th, and the following morning the movement up the Rosebud commenced; the command having been divided into two parts, one of cavalry the other of infantry, the latter composed of the battalions of the Fifth, Sixth, Seventh, and Twenty-second. We started at 5 A M., but the day was exceedingly hot and our march was very slow, as heavy parties had to be constantly engaged repairing the road for our wagons, so that we made only between nine and ten miles. The next day the weather turned very cold, overcoats and fires were comfortable, and we made only nine miles and a half after working all day on the road.

Crow scouts had been sent out on the 8th to try and communicate with General Crook, but they showed great reluctance to go far from the column, and on the 10th came running into the command uttering loud yells and saying the Sioux were coming. The scene was striking, and soon became exciting. Along through the valley, here wide and open, our straggling train was making its way flanked on each side by a line of infantry skirmishers. The advance had just passed over a hill from the top of which a good view of the surrounding country was presented. The Crows in parties of twos and threes came riding down the valley at full speed, uttering the most piercing yells, and every now and then circling around to announce the enemy in sight. They presented every appearance of running away, and nothing could stop them until they had passed considerably to the rear of the advance troops. But on the top of the hill where I was standing they met their packhorses, extra ponies, conducted by their squaws and the hangers-on of the camp, and now was seen the object of their hasty retreat. Leaping from his panting steed each warrior commenced to strip for the fight. Shirts, leggings, saddles, etc., were rapidly pulled off and thrown upon the ground, to be hurriedly picked up by the now equally excited squaws, who, with loud cries, packed them away on the backs of the already loaded horses here, there, or anywhere, and in an incredibly short space of time the men, mounted barebacked and rifle in hand, were off like the wind for the front again. On our right was the brush-fringed bed of the stream, beyond which the ground sloped gradually up towards a high ridge which ran obliquely across our front towards a point projecting out into the valley. Beyond this point where the stream (if that can be called a *stream* which is composed of stagnant pools of dirty alkali water) appeared to bend to the right, the Indians pointed excitedly to a column of smoke or dust rising above the hilltop. Whilst looking at this and speculating as to what might be causing it, my attention was attracted by two horsemen coming at full speed down the slope of the ridge on our right. On reaching the more level ground below, their horses suddenly changed direction, and wheeling twice in a circle still at full speed continued on towards us, the riders' shrill cries echoing over the valley. These discordant sounds startled a deer from his quiet bed in the valley, and our attention was for a moment attracted by a splendid buck, who went bounding across the valley before the two horsemen, as if dear life depended on his speed. These two scouts coming from the top of the ridge where they could command a view beyond, seemed to decide the question in regard to the near presence of a foe; and preparations were at once made to meet him. The train was rapidly closed up and parked in a convenient place, the leading cavalry deployed in line and pushed forward up the valley, and the infantry in lines of skirmishers on each flank. As the cavalry moved out, opening like a vast fan across the valley, General Terry moved with his staff to the front, and almost immediately a ringing cheer, reminding of war-times long past, broke from the whole line. Still no shots were heard, and we were not long left in doubt, for the Crows came riding back, calling out at the top of their voices, "Maschetee, maschetee" *(soldiers)*, and we knew that all this dust and turmoil was caused by friends instead of foes, and that General Crook and not Sitting Bull was approaching. As the cavalry was deployed to the front the line encountered a single individual riding towards it at a gallop, his long hair streaming in the wind, and as the men recognized "Buffalo Bill" they broke out in loud cheers of welcome. He announced the near approach of General Crook's troops, and soon afterwards the junction between the two forces was accomplished.

General Crook's column was on a large Indian trail which had been followed for some distance down the Rosebud. Just where our two forces joined, the trail left the valley of the Rosebud, and turned eastward towards Tongue River. Several rains had fallen upon the trail, and the guides differed in regard to its age. But the fact was apparent that the whole hostile force had eluded the two columns, and made, for the present, its escape eastward. The presence of Indians at the mouth of Powder River during the first of the month now became strongly significant, and it was to be feared that, as they had gotten such a start, they would succeed in getting across the Yellowstone, and proceed north before we could catch them. Once across the Yellowstone, they would make for the Missouri River, and if pressed across that, it was but comparatively a short distance to safety, beyond the British line. Hence it was decided to push on in pursuit with the main body, sending a portion hastily back to the Yellowstone to get on board of a steamer, and patrol the lower part of that stream, and sending back also our wagons after taking from them the pack-mules and supplies needed for the trip. The force for patrolling the river started that afternoon, and the next morning our long column stretched itself out to the eastward on the Indian trail.

The well-organized pack-train of General Crook's column, with its skilled packers and trained mules, excited our admiration and envy as the well-broken animals trotted along to the sound of the bell tinkling in their front. This bell was certainly to them "good medicine," for no well-trained pack-mule will ever permit himself to be beyond the sound of that bell, and it is only necessary to sound it to assemble every mule belonging to that particular train. Very different was it with the packs belonging to the Dakota column. Most of our mules were draft animals, and had never been packed before. Our saddles were of art inferior kind, and our packers, the men themselves, generally without any experience in what is always a very delicate and skilful operation. Each individual mule had to be led by a soldier, and the obstinate traits of the animal as developed under the new and novel circumstances of the work he was called upon to perform, would have been amusing had they not been so costly. They took anything but kindly to the loosely fastened, rattling packs, threw their heels into the air, their packs over their heads, and, having thus relieved themselves from boxes of hard bread and sacks of bacon, in several instances galloped back to the wagon train, testifying by their loud and characteristic brays as they rejoined their comrades, their preference for pulling, over packs. I saw one poor fellow going down a very steep hill, his pack almost touching his long ears as the loosened fastenings permitted it to slip forward. At last, tired of his disagreeable burden, he added to the mischief by kicking up behind. The load was in such a condition as to need just this additional incentive to take its departure, and with a bound a box of hard bread broke loose, and, striking upon a corner, went rolling end over end down the steep descent until, hitting a rock harder than its contents, the box flew into a number of pieces, and a layer of "hard tack" was strewed for twenty yards down the slope.

We crossed the high rolling divide separating the Rosebud from Tongue River, and crossing the latter stream proceeded some miles down its valley. The guides report a separation in the trail, but that of a large portion still leads down the valley, and most of the country has been recently burnt over, whilst smoke of still burning fires are seen to the eastward. We found, however, a spot where the grass was green and luxuriant, and bivouacked for the night in it. By the order regulating the movement, no canvas was permitted, no cooking utensils except tin cups, and no clothing or blankets except what each officer and man carried on his person or horse. Such deprivations would not amount to much usually in a dry, clear atmosphere like that of Montana, but old Nick himself seemed to have seized upon the weather-gauge, and that night, after making our bivouac under a clear sky, the rain commenced to fall in torrents, and it was not long before each one, from the general to the private soldier, found himself lying in a puddle of water. It rained on the just and the unjust, on the high and the low, but so far as concerns the latter, inches in altitude were of far more importance than grades in rank, and happy was he who had chosen his bed wisely, and placed his blanket on an elevation and not in a depression. 1 was not among the wise ones, and had, like most others, to turn out, or rather *up*, light a fire (no easy matter), and shiver soaking by it till daylight. I scarcely ever saw it rain more heavily anywhere than it did on us during our trip down the Tongue River. For three nights in succession everything was thoroughly soaked, and the command got but little sleep. We still pushed on down the river, cheered by the news from the scouts that the trail grew fresher, but as we neared the mouth it turned eastward again, and proceeded towards Powder River. We pushed on in pursuit, having communicated with the steamer on the Yellowstone, and ascertained that as yet no Indians had crossed the river so far as was known. We reached Powder

River on the 15th, after passing over a very rough broken country, only to find the whole country burnt over, and no Indians in sight. Twenty miles down the river we followed the trail to a point where General Terry struck it when he came from the east in June, and went into camp in the midst of a rain which came down as though a second deluge was in order. Late in the afternoon the sun burst through the thick clouds, and lighting up the still falling rain, spanned the eastern hills with a magnificent rainbow, as if giving promise of clear weather, a prognostic we were only too ready to accept as true. An incident occurred on this day's march (August 16th) which will serve to show one of the many difficulties under which military operations are conducted in a wild region like this. One of the officers, a fine young captain of infantry, suddenly fell down at the head of his company in a fit of apoplexy, or paralysis, and for weeks afterwards never spoke a word. He was perfectly helpless, and the matter of his transportation became a question of serious importance. Fortunately it was near the close of the day's march, and the distance to our camping-place was not great. But how to carry him at all was the question to be solved. The rearguard was halted, and luckily with this was Lieutenant D., whose services with the wounded of the Seventh Cavalry had proved so valuable. He set to work, and in a couple of hours constructed a litter upon which the poor sufferer was carried to camp in the midst of a pouring rain. The next day he was carried in the same way to the mouth of Powder River, and placed on board of a steamboat.

We still followed the Indian trail down Powder River, but twelve or fifteen miles from its mouth the trail suddenly turned to the eastward, and now our guides and scouts seemed to be in still greater doubt than ever regarding its age or, in other words, our proximity to the Indians. There were no indications leading to the belief that we were anywhere close to them, and whilst scouting parties were sent far ahead on the trail, the command marched to the mouth of the Powder to obtain supplies, more especially forage for our animals, many of which were becoming worn down and weak from hard travel and the lack of sufficient food.

The mouth of the Powder is a bleak, desolate region, with poor grass, much of which had been burnt off by the Indians, but by scattering the command along the valley some grazing was obtained, and, with what grain we could get, our horses and mules began to pick up their strength. Here we remained a week, our wagon train and supplies being brought down in the meantime from the mouth of the Rosebud. Of these seven days, we were deluged during three with heavy rains, notwithstanding our promising bow on the 16th.

During the latter part of this march our Crow allies began to show signs of impatience, and a desire to leave us and return to their tribe. This, in view of our future operations, and their excellent qualities as scouts, would prove a serious loss to us. But they had already served a longer time than they had originally engaged for, and it was difficult to see if they demanded their discharge how it could be refused.

One day, seated with my back against a post, pencilling a letter, the whole delegation, squaws and all, approached the spot, but with no interpreter, and whilst I was wondering what was going to take place, the party formed a circle round me and the leader advancing, gravely took my cap from my head and placed it in my lap, solemnly placed one hand upon my scalp as though blessing me, and with the other grasped my hand, shook it and retired. This ceremony was performed in solemn silence by each of the warriors belonging to the band, and I came to the conclusion that they were going to leave us, and were desirous of securing my scalp upon my head for the future. An interpreter being summoned, they expressed through him their desire to return to their people to make provision for the coming winter, by killing buffalo for their women and children, and I found that the ceremony they had gone through signified a *petition* that I would grant their request and discharge them. They expressed great and sincere devotion to our service and a desire to join us again in fighting their enemies, the Sioux. I promised to intercede with General Terry in their favor, and two days afterwards (August 20th) they were discharged and left us with the regrets of all, for we had become much attached to them, and deplored the loss of such faithful and intelligent scouts.

On the 24th, the recuperated command started up Powder River, to take up again the abandoned Indian trail; but the next day "Buffalo Bill" overtook us with a dispatch announcing the approach of steamers with more troops on board, and that they had been fired into by Indians lower down the Yellowstone. This, coupled with the report, received two days before, that Indians were crossing the river above Fort Buford, gave rise to the impression that they were endeavoring to escape to the north, and caused a change of programme. Hence it was decided to divide the command, and, whilst General Crook followed the Indian trail, our column retraced its steps, struck across the country, and the next day (26th) reached the Yellowstone lower down, near the mouth of O'Fallon's Creek. The next morning two steamers arrived, and the command was at once ferried across the river, and late in the afternoon, with pack-mules and in light, very light, marching order, started out for a night-march to the northward. Now it was that we felt the great want of our Crow allies, for this region of country was totally unknown to us. We had no guides with us who knew anything about it, and those we had declared that in all probability, from the lay of the country, we should find no water. The peninsula lying between the Missouri and Yellowstone Rivers, here something over one hundred miles wide, is known to by a high rolling divide, intersected by but few streams, and these generally dry in summer. But Big Dry Creek, a tributary of the Missouri, to the westward of us, was known to be the favorite location of Sitting Bull's camp, and running to it along on the south of the Missouri River, a lodge-pole trail was known to exist. Should the hostiles succeed in crossing the Yellowstone, they would, in all probability, use this trail. To strike it, and if possible any Indians who might be moving on it, was the object of our present movement.

We marched till a late hour of the night, bivouacked in the hills without water, and early the next morning resumed the march without breakfast. The luxuriant growth of grass in the country we passed over, probably the result of the unusually copious falls of rain during the summer, encouraged us in the hope of being able to find water for drinking purposes, and we had not proceeded many miles before the scouts reported they had discovered some pools in the bed of Bad Route Creek, a short distance ahead. Towards these the march was at once directed, and although the first pools discovered were merely small *mud-puddles,* preparations were at once made to utilize these for the manufacture of coffee. Further search, however, developed the existence of a plentiful supply of clear water in large pools, and the whole command enjoyed a hearty breakfast with coffee, for without the latter a soldier's breakfast is but a poor concern. Then, after a halt of a couple of hours, the march was resumed in a direction due north. The day was intensely hot, and both men and animals suffered a good deal for want of water, but we succeeded in finding some small pools from which the men eagerly drank and filled their canteens. During the day the scouts reported buffalo in sight, and this was cheering news, for the presence of buffalo not only indicates, the existence of water in the vicinity, but is a pretty good sign generally that Indians are not far off, just as the presence of a commissary train in time of war indicates the near presence of troops. The vicinity of buffalo, however, brought us a torment in the shape of immense numbers of buffalo-gnats, which swarmed around us like bees, stinging men and horses in a way which rendered both almost frantic with pain. As the day approached its close, anxious search was made for water in every direction. The few spades with the command were produced, and with these and the invaluable trowel- bayonets carried by some of the men, holes were dug in the low places where water evidently had been at no very distant period. Not a drop, however, rewarded our labors, and our thoughts began to be seriously directed towards another dry camp, when one of the scouts reported the glad tidings of water in a ravine a mile or two ahead. That the summer's rain had left a supply of water in the country was encouraging, not only in reference to the practicability of passing through the region with a command, but in regard to the probability of finding Indians there, and raised hopes that, after all the long delay, an effectual blow might yet be struck.

The next day our march to the north was resumed over a high rolling country, well covered with rich pasturage, and we began to encounter game in abundance. Hundreds of antelope flocked around the column, and crossing a high divide we came in sight of herds of buffalo. But they were quietly feeding, and showed no indications of the proximity of Indians. Still farther to the north rose a high broken ridge of hills forming the divide between us and the Missouri River, and near this the trail of which we were in search was supposed to run. As we advanced the buffalo became more numerous, and finally the command was halted in a little valley, and permission given for the men to obtain a supply of fresh meat, of which they stood greatly in need.

Now commenced one of the most exciting scenes ever witnessed in the western country. Groups of horsemen moved out in different directions towards the herds quietly feeding on the neighboring hills. At first but little attention was paid to the approaching horsemen; for the buffalo is not usually a very watchful animal, and with the wind in your favor, you can approach them very closely before being perceived; but at length one of the herd looks up from under his shaggy brows, perceives you are not a buffalo, makes an observation to his fellows, and with a slow lumbering gait, reminding one of the awkward movements of an elephant, the whole herd moves off. The horses now strike into a trot, and then a gallop, in pursuit. The faster the horses go, the more rapid becomes the gait of the buffalo, until both pursuers and pursued are on tl\e full run, the hunted straining every nerve to get out of the way, the hunters every nerve to close upon the prey. If a descending slope is reached, especially a steep and rough one, the buffalo at once shows to advantage, and rapidly widens the gap between himself and the horsemen, but on an ascending smooth slope or on level ground, the horseman redoubles his pace and soon forges up alongside the herd. As they close up, the frightened herd scatters out, still, however, running in the same general direction; the cows and calves with loud bellows of fear dodging in and about the larger bulls to get out of the way of the dreaded danger. Each horseman now singles out his particular game, and with all speed presses his horse up alongside. A puff of white smoke is seen, followed by the sound of a pistol-shot; but still the mad race goes on ; another and another shot follows, and now all the buffalo on the surrounding slopes raise their lazy heads, become aware of their danger, recognize their dread enemy, man, and commence to move off in different directions. But they find new enemies at every step, and wild with fright rush off on any course which seems to offer safety. Ride with me to the top of this little knoll, and take a view of the field of battle. In every direction are small herds of buffalo on the full run, followed or accompanied by horsemen in twos or threes, while puffs of smoke and a constant rattle of small arms produce the impression of a bygone battlefield. Every now and then one of the black objects is seen to fall behind the herd, to stagger, sink down and throw his heels up in the air, whilst a loud shout from the victor proclaims his triumph. See that herd wild with fright rushing directly towards a horseman, who sits quietly waiting his chance with a cocked revolver in his hand. Now they approach him, and recognizing their new danger, turn aside without slackening their gait. But with a sudden dash he is abreast of them on his fresh horse; bang! bang! goes his pistol, and one of the herd rolls in the dust, while the others continue their mad flight. Look at this herd, madly tearing up this slope directly towards us, intent only upon escaping the fiends at their back, as crazy with excitement as they are with fear. They know not and care not what is ahead, but as they rise the hill and go rushing down the opposite slope, a long line of men and horses is seen to bar their way, and half dead with fright they wheel and scatter. Look out, now, for yourself, for the hunters are as mad as the hunted, and where men are rushing about with cocked revolvers in their hands there is no knowing where the bullets may go, and one which misses a buffalo may bury itself in you. Bang! bang! go the pistols close to your ear, as the frightened animals rush past you, their long tongues lolling out, and bellowing with fear, and as the field of conflict clears away, several black carcasses are seen lying on the ground close by the column of troops. The herds disappear over the hills, a distant shot is heard now and then, and the buffalo hunt is over, with enough fresh meat lying around us for a week's supply. This is quickly cut up and packed away upon our mules, and the command resumes its march, with the means, if required, of making a longer scout than was at first proposed. A detachment of cavalry is sent off towards the divide to the northward, to examine the trail, whilst the main column turns to the eastward, to camp late in the day at some stagnant water-pools, the strong smell of buffalo from which calls forth comments about living on buffalo *straight* in every form. The next day we still continued the eastward course, and were rejoined by the detached cavalry, which found the trail, but with no indications that it had been recently used, so that if any Indians have crossed to the north of the Yellowstone we are still ahead of them, and may yet strike them lower down. Scouts are now kept well out from the column, but failing to discover any signs of Indians, the command was again turned to the southward on the 31st, a large cavalry force being sent still further to the eastward, to definitely decide the question as to the presence of any Indians in that direction, and on the 3d of September, the whole force was once more concentrated on the Yellowstone near the mouth of Glendive Creek, it being now certain that no considerable body ot Indians had gone north, and eveiy one being anxious to hear whether General Crook had been any more successful on the south side of the river than we had been on the north. It was expected that General Crook's troops would come in to this point for supplies, but several days passed without hearing from them, and at length a dispatch came by courier to say that he had found the Indian trail divided, and that he was going to strike still further to the east and southward.

Our stern chase had thus proved a long and fruitless one, and we had no longer even a shifting objective point to move against; for the Indians had doubtless divided their forces in the wilderness to the south of the Yellowstone, and could at any time concentrate again or remain scattered, according to circumstances.

Orders had been received for the establishment for the winter of a large force on the Yellowstone near the mouth of the Tongue, the site of one of the proposed new posts, and for the transportation to that point of a winter's supply for fifteen hundred men. The river was now rapidly falling, and the steamboat captains expressed doubts as to whether they would be able to make many more trips up, even as far as the point we were then at. Should this prove true, then all the supplies necessary for the force to be left in the wilderness would have to be brought by wagons from Fort Buford, and in any event sent in that way from this point to the post on Tongue River. Our supply of wagon transportation was limited, and a part of that belonging to the Montana column being left for service at the new post, the Montana troops started on their homeward march on the 6th of September with twenty-five days' rations, and a march of six hundred miles ahead of them.

Our homeward march was devoid of any incident of special note, and after passing over about one hundred miles of it, we reached the point where we met General Terry on the 8th of June, and turned back up the Yellowstone. From here our route was substantially the same as the route followed down the river in the spring, except that on passing the mouth of the Big Horn River we found the Yellowstone still too high to admit of fording, and this compelled us to keep north of the river, and pass through a very rough and difficult country. In making the march the men were in much better condition for it than the horses and mules, which for six months had been hard at work on indifferent food. The men, it is true, were dirty and ragged, but their physical condition was excellent, and they got over their twenty to thirty miles a day with far more ease and comfort than the animals did. The cavalry reached Fort Ellis on the 29th of September, and the infantry striking north from a point sixty miles east of that post, arrived at Fort Shaw on the 6th of October.

During their six months' absence in the field the objects attained by them were not at all proportionate to the efforts put forth, but should any feel inclined to criticize too closely our want of success by indulging in sarcastic calculations as to how many millions of dollars are required to kill one Indian, the only answer that can be made is—the truth of which is well recognized in the army—that war is far more costly than peace, and that it never has been, and never can be, a paying speculation. Wars are always costly, and, like commercial operations, the larger the transactions the more cheaply, generally, are they conducted. And it may be safely asserted that, considering the circumstances, Indian wars are in proportion no more costly than any other kind of wars. It is very certain that in Indian wars the labor performed is far greater than in so called *civilised* wars (as if war in any shape could be called civilized!), whilst the troops engaged have not even the poor consolation of being credited with *"glory"* a term which, upon the frontier, has long since been defined to signify being "shot by an Indian from behind a rock, and having your name wrongly spelled in the newspapers!" Hence, if the American people do not wish to spend money they should not go to war. Doubtless many well- meaning people will say, "That is all very well, but how are you going to avoid it?" This question I will answer by asking another. How do you ever avoid war? It can be avoided sometimes by the exercise of a spirit of concession and justice, a spirit directly opposite to that which has universally characterized the treatment of the red man of this continent by the American people. You cannot point to one single treaty made with the Indians which has not at some time or other been violated by the whites, and you can point to innumerable instances where the Indian has been most outrageously swindled by the agents of the government; and the great wonder is, not that we have had so many wars but that we have had so few. The Indian, although a savage, is still a man, with probably quite as much instinctive sense of right and wrong as a white man, and quite as sensible as the latter when wrongs are perpetrated against him. *He* argues in this way: The white man has come into *my* country and taken away everything which formerly belonged to me. He even drives off and recklessly destroys the game which the Great Spirit has given me to subsist on. He owes me something for this, but generally refuses to pay. Now and then, as we find his

113

settlements closing in around us, we succeed in getting him to promise us a certain yearly amount of food and clothing, that our wives and children may not starve or freeze to death, but when his agents come to turn these over to ys we find the quantity growing less and less every year, and the agents growing rich upon what was intended to feed and clothe us. We try to reach the ear of our "Great Father" to tell him of our troubles, and how his agents defraud us, but *he is so fat away that our words do not reach him.* We cannot see our wives and children starve, and year by year the danger becomes greater from the constant encroachment of the whites, who insist upon settling upon the land guaranteed to us by solemn treaty. Let us go to war and force back the settlements of these intruders, or if we must die, let us die like men and warriors, not like dogs.

Let the great people of America say whether or not the Indian is logical in his savage way, or whether or not the premises from which he argues are sound. None will dispute that his country has been overrun, and taken from him for less than "a mess of pottage;" and few will deny that the game on which he depends for subsistence is recklessly destroyed by the white men, so that in a few years more it will have entirely ceased to exist. None but Indian agents and their abettors will deny the fact that, with but few exceptions, all such agents retire from their positions enriched by the spoils from the agencies, and that, although exposures of these frauds have been made over and over again, none of these government agents are ever brought to punishment, or made to disgorge their ill-gotten gains, whilst the Indians are left to suffer for the actual necessaries of life. When, then, the Indian, driven to desperation by neglect or want and his sense of wrong, goes to war (and even a Christian will fight before he will starve), the army is called in to whip "these wards of the nation" into subjection, and when the task is successfully accomplished, as it always is in the end, the same old round of deceit and fraud commences again, and continues till the next war opens; but all the blame for these expensive wars is laid upon the military, supposed, by the "Indian ring," to be so bloodthirsty as never to be contented unless engaged in the delightful (?) task of chasing roving bands of Indians for thousands of miles through a wilderness, sometimes with the mercury frozen in the tube, for the purpose of bringing into subjection a people forced into war by the very agents of the government which makes war upon them.

Let the American people remove this foul blot from their record by insisting that the red man shall be treated with something like justice, listening to the voice of reason and common humanity, and seeing to it that all the ample means provided by their liberality shall be expended on the Indians, instead of squandered and stolen under a system which is a disgrace to the age and the country. The small, miserable remnant of a race which once covered this whole continent can be retained in peaceful relations with the whites by simply expending for their benefit the funds appropriated every year by Congress. To feed and clothe them is cheaper in every way than to fight them, and if they are fed and clothed they will not fight. If, however, the people of the United States insist upon pretending to do *both,* let them cease to complain of the expense of one part of their bad system, and lay the responsibility for the results where it properly and justly belongs.

As connected with this subject of making war upon Indians, it may be not only interesting, but instructive, to glance at some of the elements involved in the struggle, and it is possible that a due appreciation of them may be - of benefit to the people at large, and aid in inducing them to avert such wars by commencing the remedy at the right point.

Of the ultimate result of the struggle between civilization and barbarism there can be no question. The complete extinction of the red man is, in the end, certain. He may succeed in averting this for a time, and by such temporary triumphs as the Fetterman and Custer massacres postpone the fatal day, but ultimately the result will surely come, and as day by day and year by year the white settlements close in around his hunting-grounds, he is gradually becoming aware of his approaching doom. In the meantime he occupies a vast territory of comparatively unexplored country, into which the troops are obliged to seek him when active hostilities open. Of the geography of this region the troops are almost completely ignorant, and are not unfrequently entirely at the mercy of incompetent guides, not only in their movements, but for the discovery of what is absolutely necessary to the success of such movements—water. Civilized warfare is conducted upon certain well- established principles, in which good maps of the country operated in constitute a very important element. In addition to which there is always a stable "objective point" to every campaign which the commander knows cannot be suddenly changed to some other place, and elude his combinations', as an Indian village does. To the Indian, every foot of the country he is operating in is as familiar as are the paths of our flower gardens to us. He has travelled and hunted over it from childhood, knows every path, every pass in the mountains, and every water-hole, as thoroughly as the antelope or other wild animals which range through it. He knows exactly where he can go and where he cannot, where troops can come and will come, and where they cannot, and he knows the points from which he can safely watch the whole country, and give timely notice of the movements of troops, and direct those of his own camps so as to avoid an encounter, or concentrate to meet one. The best horseman in the world, he can, on his fleet little pony, the speed of which is a matter of wonder to the white man, pass over incredible distances in the shortest time, his mode of life accustoming him to any amount of fatigue, and the greatest deprivations in the way of clothing and food. A piece of buffalo-meat strung to his saddle, and the lightest possible amount of clothing, suffices him day or night for weeks and even months together. With eyes, ears, and even nose always on

117

the alert, like any wild animal, he will discover signs of an approaching enemy more quickly and more certainly than can any white man, and will read the signs he meets with, as a scholar will read the page of an open book. He scents the smoke of a fire from a distance, and at early dawn will patiently watch from some prominent peak, as motionless as a bronze statue, the columns of smoke which at that time of day rise like pillars in the still clear air, and tell him whether a large force is preparing its breakfast, or some small scouting party is out looking for his village. If his quick eye encounters horse- tracks, he can tell with unerring certainty how many are in the party, whether the horses are ridden by white men or Indians; whether they are proceeding at a walk, a trot, a gallop, or a run; whether they are acting cautiously or carelessly; how many of the horses are ridden, and how many are without riders. He can tell whether the horses are tired or fresh, and whether they have travelled but a short distance or a very long one. The system of espionage of the Indians is probably the best in the world, and when time presses, and even the fleet-footed pony is not quick enough to convey information to their chiefs, they have a system of signals by using the smoke of fires, or the reflected light of the sun with mirrors, by which the necessary intelligence is given at great distances.

Whilst troops entering the hostile country are watched by such a system, *they* move along almost without eyes, nothing beyond a very short distance from the moving

118

column being seen or known, and the game of war is carried on very much on the principle of "Blindman's Buff." The Indians can always, in summer, avoid a single column, or select their own time and place for meeting it. And they never do meet it unless they are prepared and have *all* the advantages on their side. The campaign of last year fully exemplified this. Hence there are but two alternatives by which success can be attained. Operate against them in the winter-time, when their movements are restricted, their watchfulness less efficient, and any "signs" left in the snow as plainly read by a white man as by an Indian; or else have in the field a number of columns, so that the moving Indian villages cannot avoid all of them, and have these columns cooperate under some common head. Each of them being strong enough to take care of itself, the Indians, if successful in eluding one, will in all probability be encountered by one of the others. The two posts to be established in the Yellowstone country will serve as starting-points for two of these columns, and as depots of supplies and rest for all.

One other important element enters into this system of warfare, for which, as yet, no adequate provision has been made. This is the care of the wounded, who cannot, as in civilized warfare, be left in hospitals on the field of battle. An Indian is rarely defeated until he is dead, and he not only kills every one of his enemies he can find, but wreaks his vengeance on his dead body. Hence, a very small number of wounded men is sufficient to temporarily paralyze the offensive operations of a considerable body of troops. The Indians are better prepared in every way than our troops to carry off their wounded, and, as they invariably do it, we might very profitably take some lessons from them on the subject.

THE END.

BIG BYTE BOOKS is your source for great lost history!